AF540438

भगवद्गीता

BHAGAVAD GEETA

Swami Divyananda

Published by

GRAPEVINE INDIA PUBLISHERS PVT LTD

www.grapevineindia.com
Delhi | Mumbai
email: grapevineindiapublishers@gmail.com

Ordering Information:
Quantity sales: Special discounts are available on quantity purchases by corporations, associations, and others.
For details, reach out to the publisher.

First published by Grapevine India 2023

Printed at Nutech Print Services - India

CONTENTS

CHAPTER I

The Bhagavad Gita or the song of God was revealed by Lord Shree Krishna to Arjun on the threshold of the epic war of Mahabharata. A decisive war between two set of cousins the Kauravas and the Pandavas was just about to commence on the battlefield of Kurukshetra. A detailed account of the reasons which led to a war of such enormity are given under Introduction, under "The Setting of the Bhagavad Gita."

The Bhagavad Gita is primarily a conversation between Lord Shree Krishna and Arjun, though it begins with a dialogue between King Dhritarashtra and his minister Sanjay. Dhritarashtra being blind could not leave his palace in Hastinapur, but was eager to know the on goings of the battlefield.

धर्मक्षेत्रे कुरुक्षेत्रे समवेता युयुत्सवः ।

मामकाः पाण्डवाश्चैव किमकुर्वत सञ्जय ।

॥ १-१॥

Dhritarashtra said: O Sanjay, after gathering on the holy field of Kurukshetra, and desiring to fight, what did my sons and the sons of Pandu do?

दृष्ट्वा तु पाण्डवानीकं व्यूढं दुर्योधनस्तदा ।

आचार्यमुपसङ्गम्य राजा वचनमब्रवीत् ।

॥ १-२॥

Sanjay said: On observing the Pandava army standing in military formation, King Duryodhan approached his teacher Dronacharya, and said the following words.

पश्यैतां पाण्डुपुत्राणामाचार्य महतीं चमूम् ।

व्यूढां द्रुपदपुत्रेण तव शिष्येण धीमता ।

॥ १-३॥

Duryodhan said: Respected teacher! Behold the mighty army of the sons of Pandu, so expertly arrayed for battle by your own gifted disciple, the son of Drupad.

अत्र शूरा महेष्वासा भीमार्जुनसमा युधि ।
युयुधानो विराटश्च द्रुपदश्च महारथः ।
॥ १-४॥

Here in this army there are many heroic bowmen equal in fighting to Bhima and Arjuna; there are also great fighters like Yuyudhana, Virata and Drupada.

धृष्टकेतुश्चेकितानः काशिराजश्च वीर्यवान् ।
पुरुजित्कुन्तिभोजश्च शैब्यश्च नरपुङ्गवः ।
॥ १-५॥

There are also great, heroic, powerful fighters like Dhrstaketu, Cekitana, Kasiraja, Purujit, Kuntibhoja and Saibya.

युधामन्युश्च विक्रान्त उत्तमौजाश्च वीर्यवान् ।
सौभद्रो द्रौपदेयाश्च सर्व एव महारथाः ।
॥ १-६॥

There are the mighty Yudhamanyu, the very powerful Uttamauja, the son of Subhadra and the sons of Draupadi. All these warriors are great chariot fighters.

अस्माकं तु विशिष्टा ये तान्निबोध द्विजोत्तम ।

नायका मम सैन्यस्य संज्ञार्थं तान्ब्रवीमि ते ।

॥ १-७॥

O best of the brahmanas, for your information, let me tell you about the captains who are especially qualified to lead my military force.

भवान्भीष्मश्च कर्णश्च कृपश्च समितिञ्जयः ।

अश्वत्थामा विकर्णश्च सौमदत्तिस्तथैव च ।

॥ १-८॥

There are personalities like yourself, Bhisma, Karna, Krpa, Asvatthama, Vikarna and the son of Somadatta called Bhurisrava, who are always victorious in battle.

अन्ये च बहवः शूरा मदर्थे त्यक्तजीविताः ।

नानाशस्त्रप्रहरणाः सर्वे युद्धविशारदाः ।

॥ १-९॥

There are many other heroes who are prepared to lay down their lives for my sake. All of them are well equipped with different kinds of weapons, and all are experienced in military science.

अपर्याप्तं तदस्माकं बलं भीष्माभिरक्षितम् ।

पर्याप्तं त्विदमेतेषां बलं भीमाभिरक्षितम् ।

॥ १-१०॥

Our strength is immeasurable, and we are perfectly protected by Grandfather Bhisma, whereas the strength of the Pandavas, carefully protected by Bhima, is limited.

अयनेषु च सर्वेषु यथाभागमवस्थिताः ।

भीष्ममेवाभिरक्षन्तु भवन्तः सर्व एव हि ।

॥ १-११॥

Now all of you must give full support to Grandfather Bhisma, standing at your respective strategic points in the phalanx of the army.

तस्य सञ्जनयन्हर्षं कुरुवृद्धः पितामहः ।

सिंहनादं विनद्योच्चैः शङ्खं दध्मौ प्रतापवान् ।

॥ १-१२॥

Then Bhisma, the great valiant grandsire of the Kuru dynasty, the grandfather of the fighters, blew his conchshell very loudly like the sound of a lion, giving Duryodhana joy.

ततः शङ्खाश्च भेर्यश्च पणवानकगोमुखाः ।

सहसैवाभ्यहन्यन्त स शब्दस्तुमुलोऽभवत् ।

॥ १-१३॥

Thereafter, conches, kettledrums, bugles, trumpets, and horns suddenly blared forth, and their combined sound was overwhelming.

ततः श्वेतैर्हयैर्युक्ते महति स्यन्दने स्थितौ ।

माधवः पाण्डवश्चैव दिव्यौ शङ्खौ प्रदध्मतुः ।

॥ १-१४॥

Then, from amidst the Pandava army, seated in a glorious chariot drawn by white horses, Madhav and Arjun blew their Divine conch shells.

पाञ्चजन्यं हृषीकेशो देवदत्तं धनञ्जयः ।

पौण्ड्रं दध्मौ महाशङ्खं भीमकर्मा वृकोदरः ।

॥ १-१५॥

Hrishikesh blew his conch shell, called Panchajanya, and Arjun blew the Devadutta. Bheem, the voracious eater and performer of herculean tasks, blew his mighty conch, called Paundra.

अनन्तविजयं राजा कुन्तीपुत्रो युधिष्ठिरः ।
नकुलः सहदेवश्च सुघोषमणिपुष्पकौ
॥ १-१६॥

काश्यश्च परमेष्वासः शिखण्डी च महारथः ।
धृष्टद्युम्नो विराटश्च सात्यकिश्चापराजितः
॥ १-१७॥

द्रुपदो द्रौपदेयाश्च सर्वशः पृथिवीपते ।
सौभद्रश्च महाबाहुः शङ्खान्दध्मुः पृथक्पृथक्
॥१-१८॥

King Yudhisthira, the son of Kunti, blew his conchshell, the Anantavijaya, and Nakula and Sahadeva blew the Sughosa and Manipuspaka.

That great archer the King of Kasi, the great fighter Sikhandi, Dhrstadyumna, Virata and the unconquerable Satyaki, Drupada, the sons of Draupadi, and the others, O King, such as the son of Subhadra, greatly armed, all blew their respective conchshells.

स घोषो धार्तराष्ट्राणां हृदयानि व्यदारयत् ।

नभश्च पृथिवीं चैव तुमुलोऽभ्यनुनादयन् ।

॥ १-१९॥

The terrific sound thundered across the sky and the earth, and shattered the hearts of your sons, O Dhritarasthra.

हृषीकेशं तदा वाक्यमिदमाह महीपते ।

अर्जुन उवाच ।

सेनयोरुभयोर्मध्ये रथं स्थापय मेऽच्युत ।

॥ १-२१॥

At that time, the son of Pandu, Arjun, who had the insignia of Hanuman on the flag of his chariot, took up his bow. Seeing your sons arrayed against him, O King, Arjun then spoke the following words to Shree Krishna.

यावदेतान्निरीक्षेऽहं योद्धुकामानवस्थितान् ।

कैर्मया सह योद्धव्यमस्मिन् रणसमुद्यमे ।

॥ १-२२॥

Arjun said: O Infallible One, please take my chariot to the middle of both armies, so that I may look at the warriors arrayed for battle, whom I must fight in this great combat.

योत्स्यमानानवेक्षेऽहं य एतेऽत्र समागताः ।

धार्तराष्ट्रस्य दुर्बुद्धेर्युद्धे प्रियचिकीर्षवः ।

॥ १-२३॥

Let me see those who have come here to fight, wishing to please the evil-minded son of Dhrtarastra.

एवमुक्तो हृषीकेशो गुडाकेशेन भारत ।

सेनयोरुभयोर्मध्ये स्थापयित्वा रथोत्तमम् ।

॥ १-२४॥

Sanjay said: O Dhritarasthra, having thus been addressed by Arjun, the conqueror of sleep, Shree Krishna then drew the magnificent chariot between the two armies.

भीष्मद्रोणप्रमुखतः सर्वेषां च महीक्षिताम् ।
उवाच पार्थ पश्यैतान्समवेतान्कुरूनिति ।

॥ १-२५॥

In the presence of Bhisma, Drona and all other chieftains of the world, Hrsikesa, the Lord, said, Just behold, Partha, all the Kurus who are assembled here.

तत्रापश्यत्स्थितान्पार्थः पितॄनथ पितामहान् ।
आचार्यान्मातुलान्भ्रातॄन्पुत्रान्पौत्रान्सखींस् ।

॥ १-२६॥

There Arjuna could see, within the midst of the armies of both parties, his fathers, grandfathers, teachers, maternal uncles, brothers, sons, grandsons, friends, and also his father-in-law and well-wishers-all present there.

श्वशुरान्सुहृदश्चैव सेनयोरुभयोरपि ।
तान्समीक्ष्य स कौन्तेयः सर्वान्बन्धूनवस् ।

॥ १-२७॥

When the son of Kunti, Arjuna, saw all these different grades of friends and relatives, he became overwhelmed with compassion and spoke thus:

कृपया परयाविष्टो विषीदन्निदमब्रवीत् ।

अर्जुन उवाच ।

दृष्ट्वेमं स्वजनं कृष्ण युयुत्सुं समुपस्थितम् ।

॥ १-२८॥

Arjuna said: My dear Krsna, seeing my friends and relatives present before me in such a fighting spirit, I feel the limbs of my body quivering and my mouth drying up.

सीदन्ति मम गात्राणि मुखं च परिशुष्यति ।

वेपथुश्च शरीरे मे रोमहर्षश्च जायते ।

॥ १-२९॥

My whole body is trembling, and my hair is standing on end. My bow Gandiva is slipping from my hand, and my skin is burning.

गाण्डीवं स्रंसते हस्तात्त्वक्चैव परिदह्यते ।

न च शक्नोम्यवस्थातुं भ्रमतीव च मे मनः ।

॥ १-३०॥

I am now unable to stand here any longer. I am forgetting myself, and my mind is reeling. I foresee only evil, O killer of the Kesi demon.

निमित्तानि च पश्यामि विपरीतानि केशव ।

न च श्रेयोऽनुपश्यामि हत्वा स्वजनमाहवे ।

॥ १-३१॥

I do not see how any good can come from killing my own kinsmen in this battle, nor can I, my dear Krishna, desire any subsequent victory, kingdom, or happiness.

न काङ्क्षे विजयं कृष्ण न च राज्यं सुखानि च ।

किं नो राज्येन गोविन्द किं भोगैर्जीवितेन वा ।

॥१-३२॥

येषामर्थे काङ्क्षितं नो राज्यं भोगाः सुखानि च ।

त इमेऽवस्थिता युद्धे प्राणांस्त्यक्त्वा धनानि च ।

॥ १-३३॥

O Krishna, I do not desire the victory, kingdom, or the happiness accruing it.

Of what avail will be a kingdom, pleasures, or even life itself, when the very persons for whom we covet them, are standing before us for battle?

आचार्याः पितरः पुत्रास्तथैव च पितामहाः ।

मातुलाः श्वशुराः पौत्राः श्यालाः सम्बन्धिनस्तथा ।

॥ १-३४॥

एतान्न हन्तुमिच्छामि घ्नतोऽपि मधुसूदन ।

अपि त्रैलोक्यराज्यस्य हेतोः किं नु महीकृते ।

॥ १-३५॥

Teachers, fathers, sons, grandfathers, maternal uncles, grandsons, fathers-in-law, grand-nephews, brothers-in-law, and other kinsmen are present here, staking their lives and riches.

O Madhusudan, I do not wish to slay them, even if they attack me. If we kill the sons of Dhritarashtra, what satisfaction will we derive from the dominion over the three worlds, what to speak of this Earth?

निहत्य धार्तराष्ट्रान्नः का प्रीतिः स्याज्जनार्दन ।

पापमेवाश्रयेदस्मान्हत्वैतानाततायिनः

॥ १-३६॥

Sin will overcome us if we slay such aggressors. Therefore it is not proper for us to kill the sons of Dhrtarastra and our friends. What should we gain, O Krsna, husband of the goddess of fortune, and how could we be happy by killing our own kinsmen?

तस्मान्नार्हा वयं हन्तुं धार्तराष्ट्रान्स्वबान्धवान् ।

स्वजनं हि कथं हत्वा सुखिनः स्याम माधव

॥ १-३७॥

यद्यप्येते न पश्यन्ति लोभोपहतचेतसः ।

कुलक्षयकृतं दोषं मित्रद्रोहे च पातकम्

॥ १-३८॥

O Janardana, although these men, overtaken by greed, see no fault in killing one's family or quarreling with friends, why should we, with knowledge of the sin, engage in these acts?

कथं न ज्ञेयमस्माभिः पापादस्मान्निवर्तितुम् ।

कुलक्षयकृतं दोषं प्रपश्यद्भिर्जनार्दन

॥ १-३९॥

With the destruction of dynasty, the eternal family tradition is vanquished, and thus the rest of the family becomes involved in irreligious practice.

कुलक्षये प्रणश्यन्ति कुलधर्माः सनातनाः ।

धर्मे नष्टे कुलं कृत्स्नमधर्मोऽभिभवत्युत

॥ १-४०॥

When irreligion is prominent in the family, O Krsna, the women of the family become corrupt, and from the degradation of womanhood, O descendant of Vrsni, comes unwanted progeny.

अधर्माभिभवात्कृष्ण प्रदुष्यन्ति कुलस्त्रियः ।

स्त्रीषु दुष्टासु वार्ष्णेय जायते वर्णसङ्करः

॥ १-४१ ॥

When there is increase of unwanted population, a hellish situation is created both for the family and for those who destroy the family tradition. In such corrupt families, there is no offering of oblations of food and water to the ancestors.

सङ्करो नरकायैव कुलघ्नानां कुलस्य च ।

पतन्ति पितरो ह्येषां लुप्तपिण्डोदकक्रियाः

॥ १-४२ ॥

Due to the evil deeds of the destroyers of family tradition, all kinds of community projects and family welfare activities are devastated.

दोषैरेतैः कुलघ्नानां वर्णसङ्करकारकैः ।
उत्साद्यन्ते जातिधर्माः कुलधर्माश्च शाश्वताः
॥ १-४३॥

Through the evil deeds of those who destroy the family tradition and thus give rise to unwanted progeny, a variety of social and family welfare activities are ruined.

उत्सन्नकुलधर्माणां मनुष्याणां जनार्दन ।
नरके नियतं वासो भवतीत्यनुशुश्रुम
॥ १-४४॥

O Janardan (Krishna), I have heard from the learned that those who destroy family traditions dwell in hell for an indefinite period of time.

अहो बत महत्पापं कर्तुं व्यवसिता वयम् ।

यद्राज्यसुखलोभेन हन्तुं स्वजनमुद्यताः

॥ १-४५॥

I would consider it better for the sons of Dhrtarastra to kill me unarmed and unresisting, rather than fight with them.

यदि मामप्रतीकारमशस्त्रं शस्त्रपाणयः ।

धार्तराष्ट्रा रणे हन्युस्तन्मे क्षेमतरं भवेत्

॥ १-४६॥

Sanjaya said: Arjuna, having thus spoken on the battlefield, cast aside his bow and arrows and sat down on the chariot, his mind overwhelmed with grief.

HERE ENDETH CHAPTER I OF THE BHAGAVAD-GITA.

CHAPTER II

In this chapter, Arjun reiterates his utter inability to cope with the situation he finds himself in, and refuses to perform his duty in the impending battle. He then formally asks Shree Krishna to be his spiritual teacher.

The Supreme Lord begins imparting him divine knowledge by teaching him about the immortal nature of the self, which is not destroyed when the body is destroyed.It merely changes bodies from lifetime to lifetime, just as a person puts on new garments and discards the old ones. He reminds Arjun of his duty as a warrior, which is to fight for upholding righteousness.

Having motivated Arjun from the mundane level, Shree Krishna moves deeper into the science of work. He asks Arjun to work without attachment to the fruits of his actions. He terms the science of working without desire for rewards as buddhi-yog, or yog of the intellect.

By acting in such consciousness, bondage-creating karmas will be transformed into bondage-breaking karmas, and Arjun will attain the state beyond sorrows.

सञ्जय उवाच ।

Sānkhya Yog

एवमुक्त्वार्जुनः सङ्ख्ये रथोपस्थ उपाविशत् ।

विसृज्य सशरं चापं शोकसंविग्नमानसः

॥ १-४७॥

ॐ तत्सदिति श्रीमद्भगवद्गीतासूपनिषत्सु

ब्रह्मविद्यायां योगशास्त्रे श्रीकृष्णार्जुनसंवादे

अर्जुनविषादयोगो नाम प्रथमोऽध्यायः

॥ १॥

अथ द्वितीयोऽध्यायः । साङ्ख्ययोगः

तं तथा कृपयाविष्टमश्रुपूर्णाकुलेक्षणम् ।

विषीदन्तमिदं वाक्यमुवाच मधुसूदनः

॥ २-१॥

Sanjay said: Seeing Arjun overwhelmed with pity, his mind grief-stricken, and his eyes full of tears, Shree Krishna spoke the following words.

श्रीभगवानुवाच ।

कुतस्त्वा कश्मलमिदं विषमे समुपस्थितम् ।

अनार्यजुष्टमस्वर्ग्यमकीर्तिकरमर्जुन

॥ २-२॥

The Supreme Person [Bhagavan] said: My dear Arjuna, how have these impurities come upon you? They are not at all befitting a man who knows the progressive values of life. They do not lead to higher planets, but to infamy.

क्लैब्यं मा स्म गमः पार्थ नैतत्त्वय्युपपद्यते ।

क्षुद्रं हृदयदौर्बल्यं त्यक्त्वोत्तिष्ठ परन्तप

॥ २-३॥

O son of Prtha, do not yield to this degrading impotence. It does not become you. Give up such petty weakness of heart and arise, O chastiser of the enemy!

अर्जुन उवाच ।

कथं भीष्ममहं सङ्ख्ये द्रोणं च मधुसूदन ।

इषुभिः प्रतियोत्स्यामि पूजार्हावरिसूदन

॥ २-४॥

Arjun said: O Madhusudan, how can I shoot arrows in battle on men like Bheeshma and Dronacharya, who are worthy of my worship, O destroyer of enemies?

गुरून्हत्वा हि महानुभावान्

श्रेयो भोक्तुं भैक्ष्यमपीह लोके ।

हत्वार्थकामांस्तु गुरूनिहैव

भुञ्जीय भोगान् रुधिरप्रदिग्धान्

॥ २-५॥

It would be better to live in this world by begging, than to enjoy life by killing these noble elders, who are my teachers. If we kill them, the wealth and pleasures we enjoy will be tainted with blood.

न चैतद्विद्मः कतरन्नो गरीयो

यद्वा जयेम यदि वा नो जयेयुः ।

यानेव हत्वा न जिजीविषामस्-

तेऽवस्थिताः प्रमुखे धार्तराष्ट्राः

॥ २-६॥

We do not even know which result of this war is preferable for us—conquering them or being conquered by them. Even after killing them we will not desire to live. Yet they have taken the side of Dhritarasthra, and now stand before us on the battlefield.

कार्पण्यदोषोपहतस्वभावः

पृच्छामि त्वां धर्मसम्मूढचेताः ।

यच्छ्रेयः स्यान्निश्चितं ब्रूहि तन्मे

शिष्यस्तेऽहं शाधि मां त्वां प्रपन्नम्

॥ २-७॥

Now I am confused about my duty and have lost all composure because of weakness. In this condition I am asking You to tell me clearly what is best for me. Now I am Your disciple, and a soul surrendered unto You. Please instruct me.

न हि प्रपश्यामि ममापनुद्याद्

यच्छोकमुच्छोषणमिन्द्रियाणाम्

अवाप्य भूमावसपत्नमृद्धं

राज्यं सुराणामपि चाधिपत्यम्

॥ २-८॥

I can find no means to drive away this grief which is drying up my senses. I will not be able to destroy it even if I win an unrivalled kingdom on the earth with sovereignty like that of the demigods in heaven.

सञ्जय उवाच ।

एवमुक्त्वा हृषीकेशं गुडाकेशः परन्तप ।

न योत्स्य इति गोविन्दमुक्त्वा तूष्णीं बभूव ह

॥ २-९॥

Sanjaya said: Having spoken thus, Arjuna, chastiser of enemies, told Krishna, Govinda, I shall not fight, and fell silent.

तमुवाच हृषीकेशः प्रहसन्निव भारत ।

सेनयोरुभयोर्मध्ये विषीदन्तमिदं वचः

॥ २-१०॥

O descendant of Bharata, at that time Krsna, smiling, in the midst of both the armies, spoke the following words to the grief-stricken Arjuna.

श्रीभगवानुवाच ।

अशोच्यानन्वशोचस्त्वं प्रज्ञावादांश्च भाषसे ।

गतासूनगतासूंश्च नानुशोचन्ति पण्डिताः

॥ २-११॥

The Supreme Lord said: While you speak words of wisdom, you are mourning for that which is not worthy of grief. The wise lament neither for the living nor for the dead.

न त्वेवाहं जातु नासं न त्वं नेमे जनाधिपाः ।

न चैव न भविष्यामः सर्वे वयमतः परम्

॥ २-१२॥

Never was there a time when I did not exist, nor you, nor all these kings; nor in the future shall any of us cease to be.

देहिनोऽस्मिन्यथा देहे कौमारं यौवनं जरा ।
तथा देहान्तरप्राप्तिर्धीरस्तत्र न मुह्यति

॥ २-१३॥

Just as the embodied soul continuously passes from childhood to youth to old age, similarly, at the time of death, the soul passes into another body. The wise are not deluded by this.

मात्रास्पर्शास्तु कौन्तेय शीतोष्णसुखदुःखदाः ।
आगमापायिनोऽनित्यास्तांस्तितिक्षस्व भारत

॥ २-१४॥

O son of Kunti, the contact between the senses and the sense objects gives rise to fleeting perceptions of happiness and distress. These are non-permanent, and come and go like the winter and summer seasons. O descendent of Bharat, one must learn to tolerate them without being disturbed.

यं हि न व्यथयन्त्येते पुरुषं पुरुषर्षभ ।
समदुःखसुखं धीरं सोऽमृतत्वाय कल्पते

॥ २-१५॥

O Arjun, noblest amongst men, that person who is not affected by happiness and distress, and remains steady in both, becomes eligible for liberation.

नासतो विद्यते भावो नाभावो विद्यते सतः ।
उभयोरपि दृष्टोऽन्तस्त्वनयोस्तत्त्वदर्शिभिः

॥ २-१६॥

Those who are seers of the truth have concluded that of the nonexistent there is no endurance, and of the existent there is no cessation. This seers have concluded by studying the nature of both.

अविनाशि तु तद्विद्धि येन सर्वमिदं ततम् ।
विनाशमव्ययस्यास्य न कश्चित्कर्तुमर्हति

॥ २-१७॥

That which pervades the entire body, know it to be indestructible. No one can cause the destruction of the imperishable soul.

अन्तवन्त इमे देहा नित्यस्योक्ताः शरीरिणः ।
अनाशिनोऽप्रमेयस्य तस्माद्युध्यस्व भारत

॥ २-१८॥

Only the material body of the indestructible, immeasurable and eternal living entity is subject to destruction; therefore, fight, O descendant of Bharata.

य एनं वेत्ति हन्तारं यश्चैनं मन्यते हतम् ।
उभौ तौ न विजानीतो नायं हन्ति न हन्यते

॥ २-१९॥

He who thinks that the living entity is the slayer or that he is slain, does not understand. One who is in knowledge knows that the self slays not nor is slain.

न जायते म्रियते वा कदाचिन्

नायं भूत्वा भविता वा न भूयः ।

अजो नित्यः शाश्वतोऽयं पुराणो

न हन्यते हन्यमाने शरीरे

॥ २-२०॥

For the soul there is never birth nor death. Nor, having once been, does he ever cease to be. He is unborn, eternal, ever-existing, undying and primeval. He is not slain when the body is slain.

वेदाविनाशिनं नित्यं य एनमजमव्ययम् ।

कथं स पुरुषः पार्थ कं घातयति हन्ति कम्

॥ २-२१॥

O Partha, how can a person who knows that the soul is indestructible, unborn, eternal and immutable, kill anyone or cause anyone to kill?

वासांसि जीर्णानि यथा विहाय

नवानि गृह्णाति नरोऽपराणि ।

तथा शरीराणि विहाय जीर्णा-

न्यन्यानि संयाति नवानि देही

॥ २-२२॥

As a person puts on new garments, giving up old ones, similarly, the soul accepts new material bodies, giving up the old and useless ones.

नैनं छिन्दन्ति शस्त्राणि नैनं दहति पावकः ।

न चैनं क्लेदयन्त्यापो न शोषयति मारुतः

॥ २-२३॥

The soul can never be cut into pieces by any weapon, nor can he be burned by fire, nor moistened by water, nor withered by the wind.

अच्छेद्योऽयमदाह्योऽयमक्लेद्योऽशोष्य एव च ।

नित्यः सर्वगतः स्थाणुरचलोऽयं सनातनः

॥ २-२४॥

This individual soul is unbreakable and insoluble, and can be neither burned nor dried. He is everlasting, all-pervading, unchangeable, immovable and eternally the same.

अव्यक्तोऽयमचिन्त्योऽयमविकार्योऽयमुच्यते ।

तस्मादेवं विदित्वैनं नानुशोचितुमर्हसि

॥ २-२५॥

It is said that the soul is invisible, inconceivable, immutable, and unchangeable. Knowing this, you should not grieve for the body.

अथ चैनं नित्यजातं नित्यं वा मन्यसे मृतम् ।

तथापि त्वं महाबाहो नैवं शोचितुमर्हसि

॥ २-२६॥

If, however, you think that the soul is perpetually born and always dies, still you have no reason to lament, O mighty-armed.

जातस्य हि ध्रुवो मृत्युर्ध्रुवं जन्म मृतस्य च ।

तस्मादपरिहार्येऽर्थे न त्वं शोचितुमर्हसि

॥ २-२७॥

If, however, you think that the soul is perpetually born and always dies, still you have no reason to lament, O mighty-armed.

अव्यक्तादीनि भूतानि व्यक्तमध्यानि भारत ।

अव्यक्तनिधनान्येव तत्र का परिदेवना

॥ २-२८॥

All created beings are unmanifest in their beginning, manifest in their interim state, and unmanifest again when they are annihilated. So what need is there for lamentation?

आश्चर्यवत्पश्यति कश्चिदेन-

माश्चर्यवद्वदति तथैव चान्यः ।

आश्चर्यवच्चैनमन्यः शृणोति

श्रुत्वाप्येनं वेद न चैव कश्चित्

॥ २-२९॥

Some look on the soul as amazing, some describe him as amazing, and some hear of him as amazing, while others, even after hearing about him, cannot understand him at all.

देही नित्यमवध्योऽयं देहे सर्वस्य भारत ।
तस्मात्सर्वाणि भूतानि न त्वं शोचितुमर्हसि
॥ २-३० ॥

O descendant of Bharata, he who dwells in the body is eternal and can never be slain. Therefore you need not grieve for any creature.

स्वधर्ममपि चावेक्ष्य न विकम्पितुमर्हसि ।
धर्म्याद्धि युद्धाच्छ्रेयोऽन्यत्क्षत्रियस्य न विद्यते
॥ २-३१ ॥

Considering your specific duty as a ksatriya, you should know that there is no better engagement for you than fighting on religious principles; and so there is no need for hesitation.

यदृच्छया चोपपन्नं स्वर्गद्वारमपावृतम् ।

सुखिनः क्षत्रियाः पार्थ लभन्ते युद्धमीदृशम्

॥ २-३२॥

O Partha, happy are the ksatriyas to whom such fighting opportunities come unsought, opening for them the doors of the heavenly planets.

अथ चेत्त्वमिमं धर्म्यं सङ्ग्रामं न करिष्यसि ।

ततः स्वधर्मं कीर्तिं च हित्वा पापमवाप्स्यसि

॥ २-३३॥

If, however, you do not fight this religious war, then you will certainly incur sins for neglecting your duties and thus lose your reputation as a fighter.

अकीर्तिं चापि भूतानि कथयिष्यन्ति तेऽव्ययाम् ।

सम्भावितस्य चाकीर्तिर्मरणादतिरिच्यते

॥ २-३४॥

People will always speak of your infamy, and for one who has been honored, dishonor is worse than death.

भयाद्रणादुपरतं मंस्यन्ते त्वां महारथाः ।
येषां च त्वं बहुमतो भूत्वा यास्यसि लाघवम्

॥ २-३५॥

The great generals who have highly esteemed your name and fame will think that you have left the battlefield out of fear only, and thus they will consider you a coward.

अवाच्यवादांश्च बहून्वदिष्यन्ति तवाहिताः ।
निन्दन्तस्तव सामर्थ्यं ततो दुःखतरं नु किम्

॥ २-३६॥

Your enemies will describe you in many unkind words and scorn your ability. What could be more painful for you?

हतो वा प्राप्स्यसि स्वर्गं जित्वा वा भोक्ष्यसे महीम् ।
तस्मादुत्तिष्ठ कौन्तेय युद्धाय कृतनिश्चयः
॥ २-३७॥

O son of Kunti, either you will be killed on the battlefield and attain the heavenly planets, or you will conquer and enjoy the earthly kingdom. Therefore get up and fight with determination.

सुखदुःखे समे कृत्वा लाभालाभौ जयाजयौ ।
ततो युद्धाय युज्यस्व नैवं पापमवाप्स्यसि
॥ २-३८॥

Do thou fight for the sake of fighting, without considering happiness or distress, loss or gain, victory or defeat—and, by so doing, you shall never incur sin.

एषा तेऽभिहिता साङ्ख्ये बुद्धिर्योगे त्विमां शृणु ।

बुद्ध्या युक्तो यया पार्थ कर्मबन्धं प्रहास्यसि

॥ २-३९॥

Thus far I have declared to you the analytical knowledge of sankhya philosophy. Now listen to the knowledge of yoga whereby one works without fruitive result. O son of Prtha, when you act by such intelligence, you can free yourself from the bondage of works.

नेहाभिक्रमनाशोऽस्ति प्रत्यवायो न विद्यते ।

स्वल्पमप्यस्य धर्मस्य त्रायते महतो भयात्

॥ २-४०॥

In this endeavor there is no loss or diminution, and a little advancement on this path can protect one from the most dangerous type of fear.

व्यवसायात्मिका बुद्धिरेकेह कुरुनन्दन ।

बहुशाखा ह्यनन्ताश्च बुद्धयोऽव्यवसायिनाम्

॥ २-४१॥

Those who are on this path are resolute in purpose, and their aim is one. O beloved child of the Kurus, the intelligence of those who are irresolute is many-branched.

यामिमां पुष्पितां वाचं प्रवदन्त्यविपश्चितः ।

वेदवादरताः पार्थ नान्यदस्तीति वादिनः

॥ २-४२॥

कामात्मानः स्वर्गपरा जन्मकर्मफलप्रदाम् ।

क्रियाविशेषबहुलां भोगैश्वर्यगतिं प्रति

॥ २-४३॥

Men of small knowledge are very much attached to the flowery words of the Vedas, which recommend various fruitive activities for elevation to heavenly planets, resultant good birth, power, and so forth. Being desirous of sense gratification and opulent life, they say that there is nothing more than this.

भोगैश्वर्यप्रसक्तानां तयापहृतचेतसाम् ।
व्यवसायात्मिका बुद्धिः समाधौ न विधीयते
॥ २-४४॥

In the minds of those who are too attached to sense enjoyment and material opulence, and who are bewildered by such things, the resolute determination of devotional service to the Supreme Lord does not take place.

त्रैगुण्यविषया वेदा निस्त्रैगुण्यो भवार्जुन ।
निर्द्वन्द्वो नित्यसत्त्वस्थो निर्योगक्षेम आत्मवान्
॥ २-४५॥

The Vedas mainly deal with the subject of the three modes of material nature. Rise above these modes, O Arjuna. Be transcendental to all of them. Be free from all dualities and from all anxieties for gain and safety, and be established in the Self.

यावानर्थ उदपाने सर्वतः सम्प्लुतोदके ।
तावान्सर्वेषु वेदेषु ब्राह्मणस्य विजानतः

॥ २-४६॥

All purposes that are served by the small pond can at once be served by the great reservoirs of water. Similarly, all the purposes of the Vedas can be served to one who knows the purpose behind them.

कर्मण्येवाधिकारस्ते मा फलेषु कदाचन ।
मा कर्मफलहेतुर्भूर्मा ते सङ्गोऽस्त्वकर्मणि

॥ २-४७॥

You have a right to perform your prescribed duty, but you are not entitled to the fruits of action. Never consider yourself to be the cause of the results of your activities, and never be attached to not doing your duty.

योगस्थः कुरु कर्माणि सङ्गं त्यक्त्वा धनञ्जय ।
सिद्ध्यसिद्ध्योः समो भूत्वा समत्वं योग उच्यते

॥ २-४८॥

Be steadfast in yoga, O Arjuna. Perform your duty and abandon all attachment to success or failure. Such evenness of mind is called yoga.

दूरेण ह्यवरं कर्म बुद्धियोगाद्धनञ्जय ।
बुद्धौ शरणमन्विच्छ कृपणाः फलहेतवः

॥ २-४९॥

O Dhananjaya, rid yourself of all fruitive activities by devotional service, and surrender fully to that consciousness. Those who want to enjoy the fruits of their work are misers.

बुद्धियुक्तो जहातीह उभे सुकृतदुष्कृते ।
तस्माद्योगाय युज्यस्व योगः कर्मसु कौशलम्

॥ २-५०॥

A man engaged in devotional service rids himself of both good and bad actions even in this life. Therefore strive for yoga, O Arjuna, which is the art of all work.

कर्मजं बुद्धियुक्ता हि फलं त्यक्त्वा मनीषिणः ।
जन्मबन्धविनिर्मुक्ताः पदं गच्छन्त्यनामयम्

॥ २-५१॥

The wise, engaged in devotional service, take refuge in the Lord, and free themselves from the cycle of birth and death by renouncing the fruits of action in the material world. In this way they can attain that state beyond all miseries.

यदा ते मोहकलिलं बुद्धिर्व्यतितरिष्यति ।

तदा गन्तासि निर्वेदं श्रोतव्यस्य श्रुतस्य च

॥ २-५२॥

When your intelligence has passed out of the dense forest of delusion, you shall become indifferent to all that has been heard and all that is to be heard.

श्रुतिविप्रतिपन्ना ते यदा स्थास्यति निश्चला ।

समाधावचला बुद्धिस्तदा योगमवाप्स्यसि

॥ २-५३॥

When your mind is no longer disturbed by the flowery language of the Vedas, and when it remains fixed in the trance of self-realization, then you will have attained the Divine consciousness.

अर्जुन उवाच ।

स्थितप्रज्ञस्य का भाषा समाधिस्थस्य केशव ।

स्थितधीः किं प्रभाषेत किमासीत व्रजेत किम्

॥ २-५४॥

Arjuna said: What are the symptoms of one whose consciousness is thus merged in Transcendence? How does he speak, and what is his language? How does he sit, and how does he walk?

श्रीभगवानुवाच ।

प्रजहाति यदा कामान्सर्वान्पार्थ मनोगतान् ।

आत्मन्येवात्मना तुष्टः स्थितप्रज्ञस्तदोच्यते

॥ २-५५॥

The Blessed Lord said: O Partha, when a man gives up all varieties of sense desire which arise from mental concoction, and when his mind finds satisfaction in the self alone, then he is said to be in pure transcendental consciousness.

दुःखेष्वनुद्विग्नमनाः सुखेषु विगतस्पृहः ।
वीतरागभयक्रोधः स्थितधीर्मुनिरुच्यते
॥ २-५६ ॥

One who is not disturbed in spite of the threefold miseries, who is not elated when there is happiness, and who is free from attachment, fear and anger, is called a sage of steady mind.

यः सर्वत्रानभिस्नेहस्तत्तत्प्राप्य शुभाशुभम् ।
नाभिनन्दति न द्वेष्टि तस्य प्रज्ञा प्रतिष्ठिता
॥ २-५७ ॥

He who is without attachment, who does not rejoice when he obtains good, nor lament when he obtains evil, is firmly fixed in perfect knowledge.

यदा संहरते चायं कूर्मोऽङ्गानीव सर्वशः ।

इन्द्रियाणीन्द्रियार्थेभ्यस्तस्य प्रज्ञा प्रतिष्ठिता

॥ २-५८ ॥

One who is able to withdraw his senses from sense objects, as the tortoise draws his limbs within the shell, is to be understood as truly situated in knowledge.

विषया विनिवर्तन्ते निराहारस्य देहिनः ।

रसवर्जं रसोऽप्यस्य परं दृष्ट्वा निवर्तते

॥ २-५९ ॥

The embodied soul may be restricted from sense enjoyment, though the taste for sense objects remains. But, ceasing such engagements by experiencing a higher taste, he is fixed in consciousness.

यततो ह्यपि कौन्तेय पुरुषस्य विपश्चितः ।
इन्द्रियाणि प्रमाथीनि हरन्ति प्रसभं मनः

॥ २-६०॥

The senses are so strong and impetuous, O Arjuna, that they forcibly carry away the mind even of a man of discrimination who is endeavoring to control them.

तानि सर्वाणि संयम्य युक्त आसीत मत्परः ।
वशे हि यस्येन्द्रियाणि तस्य प्रज्ञा प्रतिष्ठिता

॥ २-६१॥

One who restrains his senses and fixes his consciousness upon Me is known as a man of steady intelligence.

ध्यायतो विषयान्पुंसः सङ्गस्तेषूपजायते ।
सङ्गात्सञ्जायते कामः कामात्क्रोधोऽभिजायते

॥ २-६२॥

While contemplating the objects of the senses, a person develops attachment for them, and from such attachment lust develops, and from lust anger arises.

क्रोधाद्भवति सम्मोहः सम्मोहात्स्मृतिविभ्रमः ।
स्मृतिभ्रंशाद् बुद्धिनाशो बुद्धिनाशात्प्रणश्यति

॥ २-६३॥

From anger, delusion arises, and from delusion bewilderment of memory. When memory is bewildered, intelligence is lost, and when intelligence is lost, one falls down again into the material pool.

रागद्वेषविमुक्तैस्तु विषयानिन्द्रियैश्चरन् ।

वियुक्तैस्तु

आत्मवश्यैर्विधेयात्मा प्रसादमधिगच्छति

॥ २-६४॥

One who can control his senses by practicing the regulated principles of freedom can obtain the complete mercy of the Lord and thus become free from all attachment and aversion.

प्रसादे सर्वदुःखानां हानिरस्योपजायते ।

प्रसन्नचेतसो ह्याशु बुद्धिः पर्यवतिष्ठते

॥ २-६५॥

For one who is so situated in the Divine consciousness, the threefold miseries of material existence exist no longer; in such a happy state, one's intelligence soon becomes steady.

नास्ति बुद्धिरयुक्तस्य न चायुक्तस्य भावना ।

न चाभावयतः शान्तिरशान्तस्य कुतः सुखम्

॥ २-६६॥

One who is not in transcendental consciousness can have neither a controlled mind nor steady intelligence, without which there is no possibility of peace. And how can there be any happiness without peace?

इन्द्रियाणां हि चरतां यन्मनोऽनुविधीयते ।

तदस्य हरति प्रज्ञां वायुर्नावमिवाम्भसि

॥ २-६७॥

As a boat on the water is swept away by a strong wind, even one of the senses on which the mind focuses can carry away a man's intelligence.

तस्माद्यस्य महाबाहो निगृहीतानि सर्वशः ।
इन्द्रियाणीन्द्रियार्थेभ्यस्तस्य प्रज्ञा प्रतिष्ठिता

॥ २-६८॥

Therefore, O mighty-armed, one whose senses are restrained from their objects is certainly of steady intelligence.

या निशा सर्वभूतानां तस्यां जागर्ति संयमी ।
यस्यां जाग्रति भूतानि सा निशा पश्यतो मुनेः

॥ २-६९॥

What is night for all beings is the time of awakening for the self-controlled; and the time of awakening for all beings is night for the introspective sage.

आपूर्यमाणमचलप्रतिष्ठं

समुद्रमापः प्रविशन्ति यद्वत् ।

तद्वत्कामा यं प्रविशन्ति सर्वे

स शान्तिमाप्नोति न कामकामी

॥ २-७०॥

A person who is not disturbed by the incessant flow of desires—that enter like rivers into the ocean which is ever being filled but is always still—can alone achieve peace, and not the man who strives to satisfy such desires.

विहाय कामान्यः सर्वान्पुमांश्चरति निःस्पृहः ।

निर्ममो निरहङ्कारः स शान्तिमधिगच्छति

॥ २-७१॥

That person, who gives up all material desires and lives free from a sense of greed, proprietorship, and egoism, attains perfect peace.

एषा ब्राह्मी स्थितिः पार्थ नैनां प्राप्य विमुह्यति ।

स्थित्वास्यामन्तकालेऽपि ब्रह्मनिर्वाणमृच्छति

॥ २-७२॥

O Parth, such is the state of an enlightened soul that having attained it, one is never again deluded. Being established in this consciousness even at the hour of death, one is liberated from the cycle of life and death and reaches the Supreme Abode of God.

ॐ तत्सदिति श्रीमद्भगवद्गीतासूपनिषत्सु

ब्रह्मविद्यायां योगशास्त्रे श्रीकृष्णार्जुनसंवादे

साङ्ख्ययोगो नाम द्वितीयोऽध्यायः

॥ २॥

अथ तृतीयोऽध्यायः । कर्मयोगः

Yea! whoso, shaking off the yoke of flesh

Lives lord, not servant, of his lusts; set free

From pride, from passion, from the sin of "Self,"

Toucheth tranquillity! O Pritha's Son!

That is the state of Brahm! There rests no dread

When that last step is reached! Live where he will,

Die when he may, such passeth from all 'plaining,

To blest Nirvana, with the Gods, attaining.

HERE ENDETH CHAPTER II OF THE BHAGAVAD-GITA.

अर्जुन उवाच ।

ज्यायसी चेत्कर्मणस्ते मता बुद्धिर्जनार्दन ।

तत्किं कर्मणि घोरे मां नियोजयसि केशव

॥ ३-१॥

Arjuna said: O Janardana, O Kesava, why do You urge me to engage in this ghastly warfare, if You think that intelligence is better than fruitive work?

व्यामिश्रेणेव वाक्येन बुद्धिं मोहयसीव मे ।

तदेकं वद निश्चित्य येन श्रेयोऽहमाप्नुयाम्

॥ ३-२॥

My intelligence is bewildered by Your equivocal instructions. Therefore, please tell me decisively what is most beneficial for me.

In this chapter, Shree Krishna explains that all beings are compelled to work by their intrinsic modes of nature, and nobody can remain without action for even a moment. Those who display external renunciation by donning the ochre robes, but internally dwell upon sense objects, are hypocrites. Superior to them are those who practice karm yog, and continue to engage in action externally, but give up attachment from within.

Shree Krishna then explains that unlike the rest of humankind, the enlightened souls who are situated in the self are not obliged to fulfill bodily responsibilities, for they are executing higher responsibilities at the level of the soul. However, if they abandon their social duties, it creates discord in the minds of common people, who tend to follow in the footsteps of the great ones.

Arjun then asks why people commit sinful acts, even unwillingly, as if by force. The Supreme Lord explains that the all-devouring sinful enemy of the world is lust alone.

CHAPTER III

श्रीभगवानुवाच ।

लोकेऽस्मिन् द्विविधा निष्ठा पुरा प्रोक्ता मयानघ ।

ज्ञानयोगेन साङ्ख्यानां कर्मयोगेन योगिनाम्

॥ ३-३॥

The Blessed Lord said: O sinless Arjuna, I have already explained that there are two classes of men who realize the Self. Some are inclined to understand Him by empirical, philosophical speculation, and others are inclined to know Him by devotional work.

न कर्मणामनारम्भान्नैष्कर्म्यं पुरुषोऽश्नुते ।

न च संन्यसनादेव सिद्धिं समधिगच्छति

॥ ३-४॥

Not by merely abstaining from work can one achieve freedom from reaction, nor by renunciation alone can one attain perfection.

न हि कश्चित्क्षणमपि जातु तिष्ठत्यकर्मकृत् ।

कार्यते ह्यवशः कर्म सर्वः प्रकृतिजैर्गुणैः

॥ ३-५॥

All men are forced to act helplessly according to the impulses born of the modes of material nature; therefore no one can refrain from doing something, not even for a moment.

कर्मेन्द्रियाणि संयम्य य आस्ते मनसा स्मरन् ।

इन्द्रियार्थान्विमूढात्मा मिथ्याचारः स उच्यते

॥ ३-६॥

One who restrains the senses and organs of action, but whose mind dwells on sense objects, certainly deludes himself and is called a pretender.

यस्त्विन्द्रियाणि मनसा नियम्यारभतेऽर्जुन ।
कर्मेन्द्रियैः कर्मयोगमसक्तः स विशिष्यते

॥ ३-७॥

On the other hand, he who controls the senses by the mind and engages his active organs in works of devotion, without attachment, is by far superior.

नियतं कुरु कर्म त्वं कर्म ज्यायो ह्यकर्मणः ।
शरीरयात्रापि च ते न प्रसिद्ध्येदकर्मणः

॥ ३-८॥

Perform your prescribed duty, for action is better than inaction. A man cannot even maintain his physical body without work.

यज्ञार्थात्कर्मणोऽन्यत्र लोकोऽयं कर्मबन्धनः ।
तदर्थं कर्म कौन्तेय मुक्तसङ्गः समाचर

॥ ३-९॥

Work done as a sacrifice for Visnu has to be performed, otherwise work binds one to this material world. Therefore, O son of Kunti, perform your prescribed duties for His satisfaction, and in that way you will always remain unattached and free from bondage.

सहयज्ञाः प्रजाः सृष्ट्वा पुरोवाच प्रजापतिः ।
अनेन प्रसविष्यध्वमेष वोऽस्त्विष्टकामधुक्

॥ ३-१०॥

In the beginning of creation, Brahma created humankind along with duties, and said, “Prosper in the performance of these yajñas (sacrifices), for they shall bestow upon you all you wish to achieve.”

देवान्भावयतानेन ते देवा भावयन्तु वः ।

परस्परं भावयन्तः श्रेयः परमवाप्स्यथ

॥ ३-११॥

By your sacrifices the celestial gods will be pleased, and by cooperation between humans and the celestial gods, prosperity will reign for all.

इष्टान्भोगान्हि वो देवा दास्यन्ते यज्ञभाविताः ।

तैर्दत्तानप्रदायैभ्यो यो भुङ्क्ते स्तेन एव सः

॥ ३-१२॥

The celestial gods, being satisfied by the performance of sacrifice, will grant you all the desired necessities of life. But those who enjoy what is given to them, without making offerings in return, are verily thieves.

यज्ञशिष्टाशिनः सन्तो मुच्यन्ते सर्वकिल्बिषैः ।

भुञ्जते ते त्वघं पापा ये पचन्त्यात्मकारणात्

॥ ३-१३

The spiritually-minded, who eat food that is first offered in sacrifice, are released from all kinds of sin. Others, who cook food for their own enjoyment, verily eat only sin.

अन्नाद्भवन्ति भूतानि पर्जन्यादन्नसम्भवः ।

यज्ञाद्भवति पर्जन्यो यज्ञः कर्मसमुद्भवः

॥ ३-१४॥

All living beings subsist on food, and food is produced by rains. Rains come from the performance of sacrifice, and sacrifice is produced by the performance of prescribed duties.

कर्म ब्रह्मोद्भवं विद्धि ब्रह्माक्षरसमुद्भवम् ।

तस्मात्सर्वगतं ब्रह्म नित्यं यज्ञे प्रतिष्ठितम्

॥ ३-१५॥

The duties for human beings are described in the Vedas, and the Vedas are manifested by God himself. Therefore, the all-pervading Lord is eternally present in acts of sacrifice.

एवं प्रवर्तितं चक्रं नानुवर्तयतीह यः ।

अघायुरिन्द्रियारामो मोघं पार्थ स जीवति

॥ ३-१६॥

O Parth, those who do not accept their responsibility in the cycle of sacrifice established by the Vedas are sinful. They live only for the delight of their senses; indeed their lives are in vain.

यस्त्वात्मरतिरेव स्यादात्मतृप्तश्च मानवः ।
आत्मन्येव च सन्तुष्टस्तस्य कार्यं न विद्यते

॥ ३-१७॥

But those who rejoice in the self, who are illumined and fully satisfied in the self, for them, there is no duty.

नैव तस्य कृतेनार्थो नाकृतेनेह कश्चन ।
न चास्य सर्वभूतेषु कश्चिदर्थव्यपाश्रयः

॥ ३-१८॥

Such self-realized souls have nothing to gain or lose either in discharging or renouncing their duties. Nor do they need to depend on other living beings to fulfill their self-interest.

तस्मादसक्तः सततं कार्यं कर्म समाचर ।

असक्तो ह्याचरन्कर्म परमाप्नोति पूरुषः

॥ ३-१९॥

Therefore, giving up attachment, perform actions as a matter of duty, for by working without being attached to the fruits, one attains the Supreme.

कर्मणैव हि संसिद्धिमास्थिता जनकादयः ।

लोकसङ्ग्रहमेवापि सम्पश्यन्कर्तुमर्हसि ॥ ३-२०॥

यद्यदाचरति श्रेष्ठस्तत्तदेवेतरो जनः ।

स यत्प्रमाणं कुरुते लोकस्तदनुवर्तते

॥ ३-२१॥

By performing their prescribed duties, King Janak and others attained perfection. You should also perform your work to set an example for the good of the world.

Whatever actions great persons perform, common people follow. Whatever standards they set, all the world pursues.

न मे पार्थास्ति कर्तव्यं त्रिषु लोकेषु किञ्चन ।

नानवाप्तमवाप्तव्यं वर्त एव च कर्मणि

॥ ३-२२॥

There is no duty for me to do in all the three worlds, O Parth, nor do I have anything to gain or attain. Yet, I am engaged in prescribed duties.

यदि ह्यहं न वर्तेयं जातु कर्मण्यतन्द्रितः ।

मम वर्त्मानुवर्तन्ते मनुष्याः पार्थ सर्वशः

॥ ३-२३॥

For if I did not carefully perform the prescribed duties, O Parth, all men would follow my path in all respects.

उत्सीदेयुरिमे लोका न कुर्यां कर्म चेदहम् ।
सङ्करस्य च कर्ता स्यामुपहन्यामिमाः प्रजाः

॥ ३-२४॥

If I ceased to perform prescribed actions, all these worlds would perish. I would be responsible for the pandemonium that would prevail, and would thereby destroy the peace of the human race.

सक्ताः कर्मण्यविद्वांसो यथा कुर्वन्ति भारत ।
कुर्याद्विद्वांस्तथासक्तश्चिकीर्षुर्लोकसङ्ग्रहम्

॥ ३-२५॥

As ignorant people perform their duties with attachment to the results, O scion of Bharat, so should the wise act without attachment, for the sake of leading people on the right path.

न बुद्धिभेदं जनयेदज्ञानां कर्मसङ्गिनाम् ।

जोषयेत्सर्वकर्माणि विद्वान्युक्तः समाचरन्

॥ ३-२६॥

The wise should not create discord in the intellects of ignorant people, who are attached to fruitive actions, by inducing them to stop work. Rather, by performing their duties in an enlightened manner, they should inspire the ignorant also to do their prescribed duties.

प्रकृतेः क्रियमाणानि गुणैः कर्माणि सर्वशः ।

अहङ्कारविमूढात्मा कर्ताहमिति मन्यते

॥ ३-२७॥

All activities are carried out by the three modes of material nature. But in ignorance, the soul, deluded by false identification with the body, thinks itself to be the doer.

तत्त्ववित्तु महाबाहो गुणकर्मविभागयोः ।
गुणा गुणेषु वर्तन्त इति मत्वा न सज्जते

॥ ३-२८॥

O mighty-armed Arjun, illumined persons distinguish the soul as distinct from guṇas and karmas. They perceive that it is only the guṇas (in the shape of the senses, mind, etc.) that move amongst the guṇas (in the shape of the objects of perception), and thus they do not get entangled in them.

प्रकृतेर्गुणसम्मूढाः सज्जन्ते गुणकर्मसु ।
तानकृत्स्नविदो मन्दान्कृत्स्नविन्न विचालयेत्

॥ ३-२९॥

Those who are deluded by the operation of the guṇas become attached to the results of their actions. But the wise who understand these truths should not unsettle such ignorant people who know very little.

मयि सर्वाणि कर्माणि संन्यस्याध्यात्मचेतसा ।

निराशीर्निर्ममो भूत्वा युध्यस्व विगतज्वरः

॥ ३-३० ॥

Performing all works as an offering unto me, constantly meditate on me as the Supreme. Become free from desire and selfishness, and with your mental grief departed, fight!

ये मे मतमिदं नित्यमनुतिष्ठन्ति मानवाः ।

श्रद्धावन्तोऽनसूयन्तो मुच्यन्ते तेऽपि कर्मभिः

॥ ३-३१ ॥

Those who abide by these teachings of mine, with profound faith and free from cavil, are released from the bondage of karma.

ये त्वेतदभ्यसूयन्तो नानुतिष्ठन्ति मे मतम् ।
सर्वज्ञानविमूढांस्तान्विद्धि नष्टानचेतसः

॥ ३-३२॥

But those who find faults with my teachings, being bereft of knowledge and devoid of discrimination, they disregard these principles and bring about their own ruin.

सदृशं चेष्टते स्वस्याः प्रकृतेर्ज्ञानवानपि ।
प्रकृतिं यान्ति भूतानि निग्रहः किं करिष्यति

॥ ३-३३॥

Even wise people act according to their natures, for all living beings are propelled by their natural tendencies. What will one gain by repression?

इन्द्रियस्येन्द्रियस्यार्थे रागद्वेषौ व्यवस्थितौ ।
तयोर्न वशमागच्छेत्तौ ह्यस्य परिपन्थिनौ

॥ ३-३४॥

The senses naturally experience attachment and aversion to the sense objects, but do not be controlled by them, for they are way-layers and foes.

श्रेयान्स्वधर्मो विगुणः परधर्मात्स्वनुष्ठितात् ।

स्वधर्मे निधनं श्रेयः परधर्मो भयावहः

॥ ३-३५॥

It is far better to perform one's natural prescribed duty, though tinged with faults, than to perform another's prescribed duty, though perfectly. In fact, it is preferable to die in the discharge of one's duty, than to follow the path of another, which is fraught with danger.

अर्जुन उवाच ।

अथ केन प्रयुक्तोऽयं पापं चरति पूरुषः ।

अनिच्छन्नपि वार्ष्णेय बलादिव नियोजितः

॥ ३-३६॥

Arjun asked: Why is a person impelled to commit sinful acts, even unwillingly, as if by force, O descendent of Vrishni (Krishna)?

श्रीभगवानुवाच ।

काम एष क्रोध एष रजोगुणसमुद्भवः ।

महाशनो महापाप्मा विद्ध्येनमिह वैरिणम्

॥ ३-३७॥

The Supreme Lord said: It is lust alone, which is born of contact with the mode of passion, and later transformed into anger. Know this as the sinful, all-devouring enemy in the world.

धूमेनाव्रियते वह्निर्यथादर्शो मलेन च ।

यथोल्बेनावृतो गर्भस्तथा तेनेदमावृतम्

॥ ३-३८॥

Just as a fire is covered by smoke, a mirror is masked by dust, and an embryo is concealed by the womb, similarly one's knowledge gets shrouded by desire.

आवृतं ज्ञानमेतेन ज्ञानिनो नित्यवैरिणा ।

कामरूपेण कौन्तेय दुष्पूरेणानलेन च

॥ ३-३९॥

The knowledge of even the most discerning gets covered by this perpetual enemy in the form of insatiable desire, which is never satisfied and burns like fire, O son of Kunti.

इन्द्रियाणि मनो बुद्धिरस्याधिष्ठानमुच्यते ।

एतैर्विमोहयत्येष ज्ञानमावृत्य देहिनम्

॥ ३-४०॥

The senses, mind, and intellect are said to be breeding grounds of desire. Through them, it clouds one's knowledge and deludes the embodied soul.

तस्मात्त्वमिन्द्रियाण्यादौ नियम्य भरतर्षभ ।

पाप्मानं प्रजहि ह्येनं ज्ञानविज्ञाननाशनम्

॥ ३-४१॥

Therefore, O best of the Bharatas, in the very beginning bring the senses under control and slay this enemy called desire, which is the embodiment of sin and destroys knowledge and realization.

इन्द्रियाणि पराण्याहुरिन्द्रियेभ्यः परं मनः ।

मनसस्तु परा बुद्धिर्यो बुद्धेः परतस्तु सः

॥ ३-४२॥

The senses are superior to the gross body, and superior to the senses is the mind. Beyond the mind is the intellect, and even beyond the intellect is the soul.

एवं बुद्धेः परं बुद्ध्वा संस्तभ्यात्मानमात्मना ।
जहि शत्रुं महाबाहो कामरूपं दुरासदम्

॥ ३-४३॥

Thus knowing the soul to be superior to the material intellect, O mighty armed Arjun, subdue the self (senses, mind, and intellect) by the self (strength of the soul), and kill this formidable enemy called lust.

ॐ तत्सदिति श्रीमद्भगवद्गीतासूपनिषत्सु
ब्रह्मविद्यायां योगशास्त्रे श्रीकृष्णार्जुनसंवादे
कर्मयोगो नाम तृतीयोऽध्यायः

॥ ३॥

अथ चतुर्थोऽध्यायः । ज्ञानकर्मसंन्यासयोगः

Fight! vanquish foes and doubts, dear Hero! Slay
What haunts thee in fond shapes, and would betray!

HERE ENDETH CHAPTER III OF THE BHAGAVAD GITA.

CHAPTER IV

In Chapter four, Shree Krishna strengthens Arjun's faith in the knowledge he is imparting to him by revealing its pristine origin. He explains how this is an eternal science that he taught in the beginning to the Sun God, and it was passed on in a continuous tradition to saintly kings.

The chapter then explains the nature of work, and discusses three principles—action, inaction, and forbidden action. It discloses how karm yogis are in the state of inaction even while performing the most engaging works, and thus, they are not entangled in karmic reactions. With this wisdom, the ancient sages performed their works, without being affected by success and failure, happiness and distress, merely as an act of sacrifice for the pleasure of God. Sacrifice is of various kinds, and many of them are mentioned here. When sacrifice is properly dedicated, its remnants become like nectar. By partaking of such nectar, performers are cleansed of impurities.

श्रीभगवानुवाच ।

इमं विवस्वते योगं प्रोक्तवानहमव्ययम् ।
विवस्वान्मनवे प्राह मनुरिक्ष्वाकवेऽब्रवीत्
॥ ४-१ ॥

The Supreme Lord Shree Krishna said: I taught this eternal science of Yog to the Sun-god, Vivasvan, who passed it on to Manu; and Manu in turn instructed it to Ikshvaku.

एवं परम्पराप्राप्तमिमं राजर्षयो विदुः ।
स कालेनेह महता योगो नष्टः परन्तप
॥ ४-२ ॥

O subduer of enemies, the saintly kings thus received this science of Yog in a continuous tradition. But with the long passage of time, it was lost to the world.

स एवायं मया तेऽद्य योगः प्रोक्तः पुरातनः ।

भक्तोऽसि मे सखा चेति रहस्यं ह्येतदुत्तमम्

॥ ४-३॥

The same ancient knowledge of Yog, which is the supreme secret, I am today revealing unto you, because you are my friend as well as my devotee, who can understand this transcendental wisdom.

अर्जुन उवाच ।

अपरं भवतो जन्म परं जन्म विवस्वतः ।

कथमेतद्विजानीयां त्वमादौ प्रोक्तवानिति

॥ ४-४॥

Arjun said: You were born much after Vivasvan. How am I to understand that in the beginning you instructed this science to him?

श्रीभगवानुवाच ।

बहूनि मे व्यतीतानि जन्मानि तव चार्जुन ।

तान्यहं वेद सर्वाणि न त्वं वेत्थ परन्तप

॥ ४-५॥

The Supreme Lord said: Both you and I have had many births, O Arjun. You have forgotten them, while I remember them all, O Parantapa.

अजोऽपि सन्नव्ययात्मा भूतानामीश्वरोऽपि सन् ।

प्रकृतिं स्वामधिष्ठाय सम्भवाम्यात्ममायया

॥ ४-६॥

Although I am unborn, the Lord of all living entities, and have an imperishable nature, yet I appear in this world by virtue of Yogmaya, my divine power.

यदा यदा हि धर्मस्य ग्लानिर्भवति भारत ।

अभ्युत्थानमधर्मस्य तदात्मानं सृजाम्यहम्

॥ ४-७॥

Whenever there is a decline in righteousness and an increase in unrighteousness, O Arjun, at that time I manifest myself on earth.

परित्राणाय साधूनां विनाशाय च दुष्कृताम् ।

धर्मसंस्थापनार्थाय सम्भवामि युगे युगे

॥ ४-८॥

To protect the righteous, to annihilate the wicked, and to reestablish the principles of dharma I appear on this earth, age after age.

जन्म कर्म च मे दिव्यमेवं यो वेत्ति तत्त्वतः ।

त्यक्त्वा देहं पुनर्जन्म नैति मामेति सोऽर्जुन

॥ ४-९॥

Those who understand the divine nature of my birth and activities, O Arjun, upon leaving the body, do not have to take birth again, but come to my eternal abode.

वीतरागभयक्रोधा मन्मया मामुपाश्रिताः ।

बहवो ज्ञानतपसा पूता मद्भावमागताः

॥ ४-१० ॥

Being freed from attachment, fear, and anger, becoming fully absorbed in me, and taking refuge in me, many persons in the past became purified by knowledge of me, and thus they attained my divine love.

ये यथा मां प्रपद्यन्ते तांस्तथैव भजाम्यहम् ।

मम वर्त्मानुवर्तन्ते मनुष्याः पार्थ सर्वशः

॥ ४-११ ॥

In whatever way people surrender unto me, I reciprocate with them accordingly. Everyone follows my path, knowingly or unknowingly, O son of Pritha.

काङ्क्षन्तः कर्मणां सिद्धिं यजन्त इह देवताः ।

क्षिप्रं हि मानुषे लोके सिद्धिर्भवति कर्मजा

॥ ४-१२ ॥

In this world, those desiring success in material activities worship the celestial gods, since material rewards manifest quickly.

चातुर्वर्ण्यं मया सृष्टं गुणकर्मविभागशः ।
तस्य कर्तारमपि मां विद्ध्यकर्तारमव्ययम्

॥ ४-१३॥

The four categories of occupations were created by me according to people's qualities and activities. Although I am the creator of this system, know me to be the non-doer and eternal.

न मां कर्माणि लिम्पन्ति न मे कर्मफले स्पृहा ।
इति मां योऽभिजानाति कर्मभिर्न स बध्यते

॥ ४-१४॥

Activities do not taint me, nor do I desire the fruits of action. One who knows me in this way is never bound by the karmic reactions of work.

एवं ज्ञात्वा कृतं कर्म पूर्वैरपि मुमुक्षुभिः ।
कुरु कर्मैव तस्मात्त्वं पूर्वैः पूर्वतरं कृतम् ॥ ४-१५॥

Knowing this truth, even seekers of liberation in ancient times performed actions. Therefore, following the footsteps of those ancient sages, you too should perform your duty.

किं कर्म किमकर्मेति कवयोऽप्यत्र मोहिताः ।

तत्ते कर्म प्रवक्ष्यामि यज्ज्ञात्वा मोक्ष्यसेऽशुभात्

॥ ४-१६॥

What is action and what is inaction? Even the wise are confused in determining this. Now I shall explain to you the secret of action, by knowing which, you may free yourself from material bondage.

कर्मणो ह्यपि बोद्धव्यं बोद्धव्यं च विकर्मणः ।

अकर्मणश्च बोद्धव्यं गहना कर्मणो गतिः

॥ ४-१७॥

You must understand the nature of all three—recommended action, wrong action, and inaction. The truth about these is profound and difficult to understand.

कर्मण्यकर्म यः पश्येदकर्मणि च कर्म यः ।

स बुद्धिमान्मनुष्येषु स युक्तः कृत्स्नकर्मकृत्

॥ ४-१८॥

Those who see action in inaction and inaction in action are truly wise amongst humans. Although performing all kinds of actions, they are yogis and masters of all their actions.

यस्य सर्वे समारम्भाः कामसङ्कल्पवर्जिताः ।

ज्ञानाग्निदग्धकर्माणं तमाहुः पण्डितं बुधाः

॥ ४-१९॥

The enlightened sages call those persons wise, whose every action is free from the desire for material pleasures and who have burnt the reactions of work in the fire of divine knowledge.

त्यक्त्वा कर्मफलासङ्गं नित्यतृप्तो निराश्रयः ।

कर्मण्यभिप्रवृत्तोऽपि नैव किञ्चित्करोति सः

॥ ४-२०॥

Such people, having given up attachment to the fruits of their actions, are always satisfied and not dependent on external things. Despite engaging in activities, they do not do anything at all.

निराशीर्यतचित्तात्मा त्यक्तसर्वपरिग्रहः ।

शारीरं केवलं कर्म कुर्वन्नाप्नोति किल्बिषम्

॥ ४-२१॥

Free from expectations and the sense of ownership, with mind and intellect fully controlled, they incur no sin, even though performing actions by one's body.

यदृच्छालाभसन्तुष्टो द्वन्द्वातीतो विमत्सरः ।

समः सिद्धावसिद्धौ च कृत्वापि न निबध्यते

॥ ४-२२॥

Content with whatever gain comes of its own accord, and free from envy, they are beyond the dualities of life. Being equipoised in success and failure, they are not bound by their actions, even while performing all kinds of activities.

गतसङ्गस्य मुक्तस्य ज्ञानावस्थितचेतसः ।

यज्ञायाचरतः कर्म समग्रं प्रविलीयते

॥ ४-२३॥

They are released from the bondage of material attachments and their intellect is established in divine knowledge. Since they perform all actions as a sacrifice (to God), they are freed from all karmic reactions.

ब्रह्मार्पणं ब्रह्म हविर्ब्रह्माग्नौ ब्रह्मणा हुतम् ।

ब्रह्मैव तेन गन्तव्यं ब्रह्मकर्मसमाधिना

॥ ४-२४॥

For those who are completely absorbed in God-consciousness, the oblation is Brahman, the ladle with which it is offered is Brahman, the act of offering is Brahman, and the sacrificial fire is also Brahman. Such persons, who view everything as God, easily attain him.

दैवमेवापरे यज्ञं योगिनः पर्युपासते ।

ब्रह्माग्नावपरे यज्ञं यज्ञेनैवोपजुह्वति

॥ ४-२५॥

Some yogis worship the celestial gods with material offerings unto them. Others worship perfectly who offer the self as sacrifice in the fire of the Supreme Truth.

श्रोत्रादीनीन्द्रियाण्यन्ये संयमाग्निषु जुह्वति ।

शब्दादीन्विषयानन्य इन्द्रियाग्निषु जुह्वति

॥ ४-२६॥

Others offer hearing and other senses in the sacrificial fire of restraint. Still others offer sound and other objects of the senses as sacrifice in the fire of senses.

सर्वाणीन्द्रियकर्माणि प्राणकर्माणि चापरे ।

आत्मसंयमयोगाग्नौ जुह्वति ज्ञानदीपिते

॥ ४-२७॥

Some, inspired by knowledge, offer the functions of all their senses and their life energy in the fire of the controlled mind.

द्रव्ययज्ञास्तपोयज्ञा योगयज्ञास्तथापरे ।

स्वाध्यायज्ञानयज्ञाश्च यतयः संशितव्रताः

॥ ४-२८॥

Some offer their wealth as sacrifice, while others offer severe austerities as sacrifice. Some practice the eightfold path of yogic practices, and yet others study the scriptures and cultivate knowledge as sacrifice, while observing strict vows.

अपाने जुह्वति प्राणं प्राणेऽपानं तथापरे ।
प्राणापानगती रुद्ध्वा प्राणायामपरायणाः

॥ ४-२९॥

And there are even others who are inclined to the process of breath restraint to remain in trance, and they practice stopping the movement of the outgoing breath into the incoming, and incoming breath into the outgoing, and thus at last remain in trance, stopping all breathing. Some of them, curtailing the eating process, offer the outgoing breath into itself, as a sacrifice.

अपरे नियताहाराः प्राणान्प्राणेषु जुह्वति ।
सर्वेऽप्येते यज्ञविदो यज्ञक्षपितकल्मषाः

॥ ४-३०॥

All these performers who know the meaning of sacrifice become cleansed of sinful reaction, and, having tasted the nectar of the remnants of such sacrifice, they go to the supreme eternal atmosphere.

यज्ञशिष्टामृतभुजो यान्ति ब्रह्म सनातनम् ।

नायं लोकोऽस्त्ययज्ञस्य कुतोऽन्यः कुरुसत्तम

॥ ४-३१॥

O best of the Kuru dynasty, without sacrifice one can never live happily on this planet or in this life: what then of the next?

एवं बहुविधा यज्ञा वितता ब्रह्मणो मुखे ।

कर्मजान्विद्धि तान्सर्वानेवं ज्ञात्वा विमोक्ष्यसे

॥ ४-३२॥

All these different types of sacrifice are approved by the Vedas, and all of them are born of different types of work. Knowing them as such, you will become liberated.

श्रेयान्द्रव्यमयाद्यज्ञाज्ज्ञानयज्ञः परन्तप ।

सर्वं कर्माखिलं पार्थ ज्ञाने परिसमाप्यते

॥ ४-३३॥

O chastiser of the enemy, the sacrifice of knowledge is greater than the sacrifice of material possessions. O son of Prtha, after all, the sacrifice of work culminates in transcendental knowledge.

तद्विद्धि प्रणिपातेन परिप्रश्नेन सेवया ।

उपदेक्ष्यन्ति ते ज्ञानं ज्ञानिनस्तत्त्वदर्शिनः

॥ ४-३४॥

Learn the Truth by approaching a spiritual master. Inquire from him with reverence and render service unto him. Such an enlightened Saint can impart knowledge unto you because he has seen the Truth.

यज्ज्ञात्वा न पुनर्मोहमेवं यास्यसि पाण्डव ।

येन भूतान्यशेषेण द्रक्ष्यस्यात्मन्यथो मयि

॥ ४-३५॥

Following this path and having achieved enlightenment from a Guru, O Arjun, you will no longer fall into delusion. In the light of that knowledge, you will see that all living beings are but parts of the Supreme, and are within me.

अपि चेदसि पापेभ्यः सर्वेभ्यः पापकृत्तमः ।
सर्वं ज्ञानप्लवेनैव वृजिनं सन्तरिष्यसि

॥ ४-३६ ॥

Even those who are considered the most immoral of all sinners can cross over this ocean of material existence by seating themselves in the boat of divine knowledge.

यथैधांसि समिद्धोऽग्निर्भस्मसात्कुरुतेऽर्जुन ।
ज्ञानाग्निः सर्वकर्माणि भस्मसात्कुरुते तथा

॥ ४-३७ ॥

As a kindled fire reduces wood to ashes, O Arjun, so does the fire of knowledge burn to ashes all reactions from material activities.

न हि ज्ञानेन सदृशं पवित्रमिह विद्यते ।
तत्स्वयं योगसंसिद्धः कालेनात्मनि विन्दति

॥ ४-३८ ॥

In this world, there is nothing as purifying as divine knowledge. One who has attained purity of mind through prolonged practice of Yog, receives such knowledge within the heart, in due course of time.

श्रद्धावाँल्लभते ज्ञानं तत्परः संयतेन्द्रियः ।

ज्ञानं लब्ध्वा परां शान्तिमचिरेणाधिगच्छति

॥ ४-३९॥

Those whose faith is deep and who have practiced controlling their mind and senses attain divine knowledge. Through such transcendental knowledge, they quickly attain everlasting supreme peace.

अज्ञश्चाश्रद्दधानश्च संशयात्मा विनश्यति ।

नायं लोकोऽस्ति न परो न सुखं संशयात्मनः

॥ ४-४०॥

But persons who possess neither faith nor knowledge, and who are of a doubting nature, suffer a downfall. For the skeptical souls, there is no happiness either in this world or the next.

योगसंन्यस्तकर्माणं ज्ञानसञ्छिन्नसंशयम् ।

आत्मवन्तं न कर्माणि निबध्नन्ति धनञ्जय

॥ ४-४१॥

O Arjun, actions do not bind those who have renounced karm in the fire of Yog, whose doubts have been dispelled by knowledge, and who are situated in knowledge of the self.

तस्मादज्ञानसम्भूतं हृत्स्थं ज्ञानासिनात्मनः ।

छित्त्वैनं संशयं योगमातिष्ठोत्तिष्ठ भारत

॥ ४-४२॥

Therefore, with the sword of knowledge, cut asunder the doubts that have arisen in your heart. O scion of Bharat, establish yourself in karm yog. Arise, stand up, and take action!

ॐ तत्सदिति श्रीमद्भगवद्गीतासूपनिषत्सु

ब्रह्मविद्यायां योगशास्त्रे श्रीकृष्णार्जुनसंवादे

ज्ञानकर्मसंन्यासयोगो नाम चतुर्थोऽध्यायः ॥ ४॥

अथ पञ्चमोऽध्यायः । संन्यासयोगः

He that, being self-contained, hath vanquished doubt,
Disparting self from service, soul from works,
Enlightened and emancipate, my Prince!
Works fetter him no more! Cut then atwain
With sword of wisdom, Son of Bharata!
This doubt that binds thy heart-beats! cleave the bond
Born of thy ignorance! Be bold and wise!

Give thyself to the field with me! Arise!

HERE ENDETH CHAPTER IV OF THE BHAGAVAD-GITA.

CHAPTER V

This chapter compares the path of karm sanyās (renunciation of actions) with the path of karm-yog (work in devotion). Shree Krishna explains that both lead to the same goal, and we can choose either of them. However, renunciation of actions cannot be done perfectly until the mind is sufficiently pure, and the purification of the mind is achieved by work in devotion. Hence, karm-yog is the appropriate option for the majority of humankind.

Karm yogis do their worldly duties with purified intellect, abandoning attachment to the fruits of their works, and dedicating them to God. Thus, they remain unaffected by sin, just as a lotus leaf remains untouched by the water on which it floats. With the light of knowledge, they realize the body to be like a city of nine gates within which the soul resides. Thus, they neither consider themselves as the doers nor the enjoyers of their actions.

Worldly people strive to relish the pleasures that arise from the sense objects, without realizing that they are verily the source of misery. But the karm yogis do not delight in them; instead they relish the bliss of God within.

अर्जुन उवाच ।

संन्यासं कर्मणां कृष्ण पुनर्योगं च शंससि ।

यच्छ्रेय एतयोरेकं तन्मे ब्रूहि सुनिश्चितम्

॥ ५-१ ॥

Arjun said: O Shree Krishna, You praised karm sanyās (the path of renunciation of actions), and You also advised to do karm yog (work with devotion). Please tell me decisively which of the two is more beneficial?

श्रीभगवानुवाच ।

संन्यासः कर्मयोगश्च निःश्रेयसकरावुभौ ।

तयोस्तु कर्मसंन्यासात्कर्मयोगो विशिष्यते

॥ ५-२ ॥

The Blessed Lord said: The renunciation of work and work in devotion are both good for liberation. But, of the two, work in devotional service is better than renunciation of works.

ज्ञेयः स नित्यसंन्यासी यो न द्वेष्टि न काङ्क्षति ।

निर्द्वन्द्वो हि महाबाहो सुखं बन्धात्प्रमुच्यते

॥ ५-३॥

One who neither hates nor desires the fruits of his activities is known to be always renounced. Such a person, liberated from all dualities, easily overcomes material bondage and is completely liberated, O mighty-armed Arjuna.

साङ्ख्ययोगौ पृथग्बालाः प्रवदन्ति न पण्डिताः ।

एकमप्यास्थितः सम्यगुभयोर्विन्दते फलम्

॥ ५-४॥

Only the ignorant speak of karma-yoga and devotional service as being different from the analytical study of the material world [sankhya]. Those who are actually learned say that he who applies himself well to one of these paths achieves the results of both.

यत्साङ्ख्यैः प्राप्यते स्थानं तद्योगैरपि गम्यते ।
एकं साङ्ख्यं च योगं च यः पश्यति स पश्यति

॥ ५-५॥

One who knows that the position reached by means of renunciation can also be attained by works in devotional service and who therefore sees that the path of works and the path of renunciation are one, sees things as they are.

संन्यासस्तु महाबाहो दुःखमाप्तुमयोगतः ।
योगयुक्तो मुनिर्ब्रह्म नचिरेणाधिगच्छति

॥ ५-६॥

Unless one is engaged in the devotional service of the Lord, mere renunciation of activities cannot make one happy. The sages, purified by works of devotion, achieve the Supreme without delay.

योगयुक्तो विशुद्धात्मा विजितात्मा जितेन्द्रियः ।
सर्वभूतात्मभूतात्मा कुर्वन्नपि न लिप्यते

॥ ५-७॥

The karm yogis, who are of purified intellect, and who control the mind and senses, see the Soul of all souls in every living being. Though performing all kinds of actions, they are never entangled.

नैव किञ्चित्करोमीति युक्तो मन्येत तत्त्ववित् ।
पश्यञ्शृण्वन्स्पृशञ्जिघ्रन्नश्नन्गच्छन्स्वपञ्श्वसन्

॥ ५-८॥

प्रलपन्विसृजन्गृह्णन्नुन्मिषन्निमिषन्नपि ।
इन्द्रियाणीन्द्रियार्थेषु वर्तन्त इति धारयन्

॥ ५-९॥

Those steadfast in this karm yog, always think, "I am not the doer," even while engaged in seeing, hearing, touching, smelling, moving, sleeping, breathing, speaking, excreting, and grasping, and opening or closing the eyes. With the light of divine knowledge, they see that it is only the material senses that are moving amongst their objects.

ब्रह्मण्याधाय कर्माणि सङ्गं त्यक्त्वा करोति यः ।

लिप्यते न स पापेन पद्मपत्रमिवाम्भसा ॥ ५-१०॥

Those who dedicate their actions to God, abandoning all attachment, remain untouched by sin, just as a lotus leaf is untouched by water.

कायेन मनसा बुद्ध्या केवलैरिन्द्रियैरपि ।

योगिनः कर्म कुर्वन्ति सङ्गं त्यक्त्वात्मशुद्धये

॥ ५-११॥

The yogis, while giving up attachment, perform actions with their body, senses, mind, and intellect, only for the purpose of self-purification.

युक्तः कर्मफलं त्यक्त्वा शान्तिमाप्नोति नैष्ठिकीम् ।

अयुक्तः कामकारेण फले सक्तो निबध्यते

॥ ५-१२॥

Offering the results of all activities to God, the karm yogis attain everlasting peace. Whereas those who, being impelled by their desires, work with a selfish motive become entangled because they are attached to the fruits of their actions.

सर्वकर्माणि मनसा संन्यस्यास्ते सुखं वशी ।
नवद्वारे पुरे देही नैव कुर्वन्न कारयन्

॥ ५-१३॥

The embodied beings who are self-controlled and detached reside happily in the city of nine gates, free from thinking they are the doers or the cause of anything.

न कर्तृत्वं न कर्माणि लोकस्य सृजति प्रभुः ।
न कर्मफलसंयोगं स्वभावस्तु प्रवर्तते

॥ ५-१४॥

Neither the sense of doership nor the nature of actions comes from God; nor does He create the fruits of actions. All this is enacted by the modes of material nature (guṇas).

नादत्ते कस्यचित्पापं न चैव सुकृतं विभुः ।
अज्ञानेनावृतं ज्ञानं तेन मुह्यन्ति जन्तवः

॥ ५-१५॥

The omnipresent God does not involve Himself in the sinful or virtuous deeds of anyone. The living entities are deluded because their inner knowledge is covered by ignorance.

ज्ञानेन तु तदज्ञानं येषां नाशितमात्मनः ।

तेषामादित्यवज्ज्ञानं प्रकाशयति तत्परम्

॥ ५-१६॥

But for those, in whom this ignorance of the self is destroyed by divine knowledge, that knowledge reveals the Supreme Entity, just as the sun illumines everything in daytime.

तदबुद्धयस्तदात्मानस्तन्निष्ठास्तत्परायणाः ।

गच्छन्त्यपुनरावृत्तिं ज्ञाननिर्धूतकल्मषाः

॥ ५-१७॥

Those whose intellect is fixed in God, who are wholly absorbed in God, with firm faith in Him as the supreme goal, such persons quickly reach the state from which there is no return, their sins having been dispelled by the light of knowledge.

विद्याविनयसम्पन्ने ब्राहमणे गवि हस्तिनि ।

शुनि चैव श्वपाके च पण्डिताः समदर्शिनः

॥ ५-१८॥

The truly learned, with the eyes of divine knowledge, see with equal vision a Brahmin, a cow, an elephant, a dog, and a dog-eater.

इहैव तैर्जितः सर्गो येषां साम्ये स्थितं मनः ।

निर्दोषं हि समं ब्रह्म तस्माद् ब्रह्मणि ते स्थिताः

॥ ५-१९॥

Those whose minds are established in equality of vision conquer the cycle of birth and death in this very life. They possess the flawless qualities of God, and are therefore seated in the Absolute Truth.

न प्रहृष्येत्प्रियं प्राप्य नोद्विजेत्प्राप्य चाप्रियम् ।

स्थिरबुद्धिरसम्मूढो ब्रह्मविद् ब्रह्मणि स्थितः

॥ ५-२०॥

Established in God, having a firm understanding of divine knowledge and not hampered by delusion, they neither rejoice in getting something pleasant nor grieve on experiencing the unpleasant.

बाह्यस्पर्शेष्वसक्तात्मा विन्दत्यात्मनि यत्सुखम् ।

स ब्रह्मयोगयुक्तात्मा सुखमक्षयमश्नुते

॥ ५-२१॥

Those who are not attached to external sense pleasures realize divine bliss in the self. Being united with God through Yog, they experience unending happiness.

ये हि संस्पर्शजा भोगा दुःखयोनय एव ते ।
आद्यन्तवन्तः कौन्तेय न तेषु रमते बुधः

॥ ५-२२॥

The pleasures that arise from contact with the sense objects, though appearing as enjoyable to worldly-minded people, are verily a source of misery. O son of Kunti, such pleasures have a beginning and an end, and so the wise do not delight in them.

शक्नोतीहैव यः सोढुं प्राक्शरीरविमोक्षणात् ।
कामक्रोधोद्भवं वेगं स युक्तः स सुखी नरः

॥ ५-२३॥

Those persons are yogis, who before giving up the body are able to check the forces of desire and anger; and they alone are happy.

योऽन्तःसुखोऽन्तरारामस्तथान्तर्ज्योतिरेव यः ।
स योगी ब्रह्मनिर्वाणं ब्रह्मभूतोऽधिगच्छति

॥ ५-२४॥

Those who are happy within themselves, enjoying the delight of God within, and are illumined by the inner light, such yogis are united with the Lord and are liberated from material existence.

लभन्ते ब्रह्मनिर्वाणमृषयः क्षीणकल्मषाः ।
छिन्नद्वैधा यतात्मानः सर्वभूतहिते रताः

॥ ५-२५॥

Those holy persons, whose sins have been purged, whose doubts are annihilated, whose minds are disciplined, and who are devoted to the welfare of all beings, attain God and are liberated from material existence.

कामक्रोधवियुक्तानां यतीनां यतचेतसाम् ।
अभितो ब्रह्मनिर्वाणं वर्तते विदितात्मनाम्
॥ ५-२६॥

For those sanyāsīs, who have broken out of anger and lust through constant effort, liberation from material existence is both here and hereafter.

स्पर्शान्कृत्वा बहिर्बाह्यांश्चक्षुश्चैवान्तरे भ्रुवोः ।
प्राणापानौ समौ कृत्वा नासाभ्यन्तरचारिणौ
॥ ५-२७॥

यतेन्द्रियमनोबुद्धिर्मुनिर्मोक्षपरायणः ।
विगतेच्छाभयक्रोधो यः सदा मुक्त एव सः
॥ ५-२८॥

Shutting out all thoughts of external enjoyment, with the gaze fixed on the space between the eye-brows, equalizing the flow of the incoming and outgoing breath in the nostrils, and thus controlling the senses, mind, and intellect, the sage who becomes free from desire and fear, always lives in freedom.

भोक्तारं यज्ञतपसां सर्वलोकमहेश्वरम् ।
सुहृदं सर्वभूतानां ज्ञात्वा मां शान्तिमृच्छति
॥ ५-२९॥

Having realized Me as the enjoyer of all sacrifices and austerities, the Supreme Lord of all the worlds and the selfless Friend of all living beings, My devotee attains peace.

ॐ तत्सदिति श्रीमद्भगवद्गीतासूपनिषत्सु
ब्रह्मविद्यायां योगशास्त्रे श्रीकृष्णार्जुनसंवादे
संन्यासयोगो नाम पञ्चमोऽध्यायः
॥ ५॥

अथ षष्ठोऽध्यायः । आत्मसंयमयोगः

That one-with organs, heart, and mind constrained,
Bent on deliverance, having put away
Passion, and fear, and rage;--hath, even now,
Obtained deliverance, ever and ever freed.
Yea! for he knows Me Who am He that heeds
The sacrifice and worship, God revealed;
And He who heeds not, being Lord of Worlds,

Lover of all that lives, God unrevealed,

Wherein who will shall find surety and shield!

HERE ENDS CHAPTER V. OF THE BHAGAVAD-GITA.

CHAPTER VI

In this chapter, Shree Krishna continues the comparative evaluation of karm yog (practicing spirituality while continuing the worldly duties) and karm sanyās (practicing spirituality in the renounced order) from chapter five and recommends the former. When we perform work in devotion, it purifies the mind and deepens our spiritual realization. Then when the mind becomes tranquil, meditation becomes the primary means of elevation.

Arjun then questions Shree Krishna about the fate of the aspirant who begins on the path, but is unable to reach the goal due to an unsteady mind. Shree Krishna reassures him that one who strives for God-realization is never overcome by evil. God always keeps account of our spiritual merits accumulated in previous lives and reawakens that wisdom in future births, so that we may continue the journey from where we had left off. The chapter concludes with a declaration that the yogi (one who strives to unite with God) is superior to the tapasvī (ascetic), the jñānī (person of learning), and the karmī (ritualistic performer). And amongst all yogis, one who engages in bhakti (loving devotion to God) is the highest of all.

श्रीभगवानुवाच ।

अनाश्रितः कर्मफलं कार्यं कर्म करोति यः ।
स संन्यासी च योगी च न निरग्निर्न चाक्रियः
॥ ६-१॥

The Supreme Lord said: Those who perform prescribed duties without desiring the results of their actions are actual sanyāsīs (renunciates) and yogis, not those who have merely ceased performing sacrifices such as agni-hotra yajña or abandoned bodily activities.

यं संन्यासमिति प्राहुर्योगं तं विद्धि पाण्डव ।
न ह्यसंन्यस्तसङ्कल्पो योगी भवति कश्चन
॥ ६-२॥

What is known as sanyās is non-different from Yog, for none become yogis without renouncing worldly desires.

आरुरुक्षोर्मुनेर्योगं कर्म कारणमुच्यते ।

योगारूढस्य तस्यैव शमः कारणमुच्यते

॥ ६-३॥

To the soul who is aspiring for perfection in Yog, work without attachment is said to be the means; to the sage who is already elevated in Yog, tranquility in meditation is said to be the means.

यदा हि नेन्द्रियार्थेषु न कर्मस्वनुषज्जते ।

सर्वसङ्कल्पसंन्यासी योगारूढस्तदोच्यते

॥ ६-४॥

When one is neither attached to sense objects nor to actions, that person is said to be elevated in the science of Yog, for having renounced all desires for the fruits of actions.

उद्धरेदात्मनात्मानं नात्मानमवसादयेत् ।

आत्मैव ह्यात्मनो बन्धुरात्मैव रिपुरात्मनः

॥ ६-५॥

Elevate yourself through the power of your mind, and not degrade yourself, for the mind can be the friend and also the enemy of the self.

बन्धुरात्मात्मनस्तस्य येनात्मैवात्मना जितः ।

अनात्मनस्तु शत्रुत्वे वर्तेतात्मैव शत्रुवत्

॥ ६-६ ॥

For those who have conquered the mind, it is their friend. For those who have failed to do so, the mind works like an enemy.

जितात्मनः प्रशान्तस्य परमात्मा समाहितः ।

शीतोष्णसुखदुःखेषु तथा मानापमानयोः

॥ ६-७ ॥

The yogis who have conquered the mind rise above the dualities of cold and heat, joy and sorrow, honor and dishonor. Such yogis remain peaceful and steadfast in their devotion to God.

ज्ञानविज्ञानतृप्तात्मा कूटस्थो विजितेन्द्रियः ।
युक्त इत्युच्यते योगी समलोष्टाश्मकाञ्चनः
॥ ६-८॥

The yogi who are satisfied by knowledge and discrimination, and have conquered their senses, remain undisturbed in all circumstances. They see everything—dirt, stones, and gold—as the same.

सुहृन्मित्रार्युदासीनमध्यस्थद्वेष्यबन्धुषु ।
साधुष्वपि च पापेषु समबुद्धिर्विशिष्यते
॥ ६-९॥

The yogis look upon all—well-wishers, friends, foes, the pious, and the sinners—with an impartial intellect. The yogi who is of equal intellect toward friend, companion, and foe, neutral among enemies and relatives, and impartial between the righteous and sinful, is considered to be distinguished among humans.

योगी युञ्जीत सततमात्मानं रहसि स्थितः ।

एकाकी यतचित्तात्मा निराशीरपरिग्रहः

॥ ६-१०॥

Those who seek the state of Yog should reside in seclusion, constantly engaged in meditation with a controlled mind and body, getting rid of desires and possessions for enjoyment.

शुचौ देशे प्रतिष्ठाप्य स्थिरमासनमात्मनः ।

नात्युच्छ्रितं नातिनीचं चैलाजिनकुशोत्तरम्

॥ ६-११॥

To practice Yog, one should make an āsan (seat) in a sanctified place, by placing kuśh grass, deer skin, and a cloth, one over the other. The āsan should be neither too high nor too low.

तत्रैकाग्रं मनः कृत्वा यतचित्तेन्द्रियक्रियः ।

उपविश्यासने युञ्ज्याद्योगमात्मविशुद्धये

॥ ६-१२॥

समं कायशिरोग्रीवं धारयन्नचलं स्थिरः ।

सम्प्रेक्ष्य नासिकाग्रं स्वं दिशश्चानवलोकयन्

॥ ६-१३॥

Seated firmly on it, the yogi should strive to purify the mind by focusing it in meditation with one pointed concentration, controlling all thoughts and activities. He must hold the body, neck, and head firmly in a straight line, and gaze at the tip of the nose, without allowing the eyes to wander.

प्रशान्तात्मा विगतभीर्ब्रह्मचारिव्रते स्थितः ।

मनः संयम्य मच्चित्तो युक्त आसीत मत्परः

॥ ६-१४॥

Thus, with a serene, fearless, and unwavering mind, and staunch in the vow of celibacy, the vigilant yogi should meditate on me, having me alone as the supreme goal.

युञ्जन्नेवं सदात्मानं योगी नियतमानसः ।
शान्तिं निर्वाणपरमां मत्संस्थामधिगच्छति

॥ ६-१५॥

Thus, constantly keeping the mind absorbed in me, the yogi of disciplined mind attains nirvāṇ, and abides in me in supreme peace.

नात्यश्नतस्तु योगोऽस्ति न चैकान्तमनश्नतः ।
न चातिस्वप्नशीलस्य जाग्रतो नैव चार्जुन

॥ ६-१६॥

O Arjun, those who eat too much or eat too little, sleep too much or too little, cannot attain success in Yog.

युक्ताहारविहारस्य युक्तचेष्टस्य कर्मसु ।
युक्तस्वप्नावबोधस्य योगो भवति दुःखहा

॥ ६-१७॥

But those who are temperate in eating and recreation, balanced in work, and regulated in sleep, can mitigate all sorrows by practicing Yog.

यदा विनियतं चित्तमात्मन्येवावतिष्ठते ।

निःस्पृहः सर्वकामेभ्यो युक्त इत्युच्यते तदा

॥ ६-१८॥

With thorough discipline, they learn to withdraw the mind from selfish cravings and rivet it on the unsurpassable good of the self. Such persons are said to be in Yog, and are free from all yearning of the senses.

यथा दीपो निवातस्थो नेङ्गते सोपमा स्मृता ।

योगिनो यतचित्तस्य युञ्जतो योगमात्मनः

॥ ६-१९॥

Just as a lamp in a windless place does not flicker, so the disciplined mind of a yogi remains steady in meditation on the self.

यत्रोपरमते चित्तं निरुद्धं योगसेवया ।

यत्र चैवात्मनात्मानं पश्यन्नात्मनि तुष्यति

॥ ६-२०॥

When the mind, restrained from material activities, becomes still by the practice of Yog, then the yogi is able to behold the soul through the purified mind, and he rejoices in the inner joy.

सुखमात्यन्तिकं यत्तद् बुद्धिग्राह्यमतीन्द्रियम् ।
वेत्ति यत्र न चैवायं स्थितश्चलति तत्त्वतः

॥ ६-२१॥

In that joyous state of Yog, called samādhi, one experiences supreme boundless divine bliss, and thus situated, one never deviates from the Eternal Truth.

यं लब्ध्वा चापरं लाभं मन्यते नाधिकं ततः ।
यस्मिन्स्थितो न दुःखेन गुरुणापि विचाल्यते

॥ ६-२२॥

Having gained that state, one does not consider any attainment to be greater. Being thus established, one is not shaken even in the midst of the greatest calamity.

तं विद्याद् दुःखसंयोगवियोगं योगसंज्ञितम् ।
स निश्चयेन योक्तव्यो योगोऽनिर्विण्णचेतसा

॥ ६-२३॥

That state of severance from union with misery is known as Yog. This Yog should be resolutely practiced with determination free from pessimism.

सङ्कल्पप्रभवान्कामांस्त्यक्त्वा सर्वानशेषतः ।

मनसैवेन्द्रियग्रामं विनियम्य समन्ततः

॥ ६-२४॥

शनैः शनैरुपरमेद् बुद्ध्या धृतिगृहीतया ।

आत्मसंस्थं मनः कृत्वा न किञ्चिदपि चिन्तयेत्

॥ ६-२५॥

Completely renouncing all desires arising from thoughts of the world, one should restrain the senses from all sides with the mind. Slowly and steadily, with conviction in the intellect, the mind will become fixed in God alone, and will think of nothing else.

यतो यतो निश्चरति मनश्चञ्चलमस्थिरम् ।

ततस्ततो नियम्यैतदात्मन्येव वशं नयेत्

॥ ६-२६॥

Whenever and wherever the restless and unsteady mind wanders, one should bring it back and continually focus it on God.

प्रशान्तमनसं ह्येनं योगिनं सुखमुत्तमम् ।

उपैति शान्तरजसं ब्रह्मभूतमकल्मषम्

॥ ६-२७॥

Great transcendental happiness comes to the yogi whose mind is calm, whose passions are subdued, who is without sin, and who sees everything in connection with God.

युञ्जन्नेवं सदात्मानं योगी विगतकल्मषः ।

सुखेन ब्रह्मसंस्पर्शमत्यन्तं सुखमश्नुते

॥ ६-२८॥

The self-controlled yogi, thus uniting the self with God, becomes free from material contamination, and being in constant touch with the Supreme, achieves the highest state of perfect happiness.

सर्वभूतस्थमात्मानं सर्वभूतानि चात्मनि ।

ईक्षते योगयुक्तात्मा सर्वत्र समदर्शनः

॥ ६-२९॥

The true yogis, uniting their consciousness with God, see with equal eye, all living beings in God and God in all living beings.

यो मां पश्यति सर्वत्र सर्वं च मयि पश्यति ।

तस्याहं न प्रणश्यामि स च मे न प्रणश्यति

॥ ६-३०॥

For those who see me everywhere and see all things in me, I am never lost, nor are they ever lost to me.

सर्वभूतस्थितं यो मां भजत्येकत्वमास्थितः ।

सर्वथा वर्तमानोऽपि स योगी मयि वर्तते

॥ ६-३१॥

The yogi who is established in union with me, and worships me as the Supreme Soul residing in all beings, dwells only in me, though engaged in all kinds of activities.

आत्मौपम्येन सर्वत्र समं पश्यति योऽर्जुन ।

सुखं वा यदि वा दुःखं स योगी परमो मतः

॥ ६-३२॥

I regard them to be perfect yogis who see the true equality of all living beings and respond to the joys and sorrows of others as if they were their own.

अर्जुन उवाच ।

योऽयं योगस्त्वया प्रोक्तः साम्येन मधुसूदन ।
एतस्याहं न पश्यामि चञ्चलत्वात्स्थितिं स्थिराम्
॥ ६-३३॥

Arjun said: The system of Yog that you have described, O Madhusudan, appears impractical and unattainable to me, due to the restless mind.

चञ्चलं हि मनः कृष्ण प्रमाथि बलवद् दृढम् ।
तस्याहं निग्रहं मन्ये वायोरिव सुदुष्करम्
॥ ६-३४॥

The mind is very restless, turbulent, strong and obstinate, O Krishna. It appears to me that it is more difficult to control than the wind.

श्रीभगवानुवाच ।

असंशयं महाबाहो मनो दुर्निग्रहं चलम् ।
अभ्यासेन तु कौन्तेय वैराग्येण च गृह्यते

॥ ६-३५॥

Lord Krishna said: O mighty-armed son of Kunti, what you say is correct; the mind is indeed very difficult to restrain. But by practice and detachment, it can be controlled.

असंयतात्मना योगो दुष्प्राप इति मे मतिः ।
वश्यात्मना तु यतता शक्योऽवाप्तुमुपायतः

॥ ६-३६॥

Yog is difficult to attain for one whose mind is unbridled. However, those who have learnt to control the mind, and who strive earnestly by the proper means, can attain perfection in Yog. This is my opinion.

अर्जुन उवाच ।

अयतिः श्रद्धयोपेतो योगाच्चलितमानसः ।

अप्राप्य योगसंसिद्धिं कां गतिं कृष्ण गच्छति

॥ ६-३७॥

Arjun said: What is the fate of the unsuccessful yogi who begins the path with faith, but who does not endeavor sufficiently, due to unsteady mind, and is unable to reach the goal of Yog in this life?

कच्चिन्नोभयविभ्रष्टश्छिन्नाभ्रमिव नश्यति ।

अप्रतिष्ठो महाबाहो विमूढो ब्रह्मणः पथि

॥ ६-३८॥

Does not such a person who deviates from Yog get deprived of both material and spiritual success, O mighty-armed Krishna, and perish like a broken cloud with no position in either sphere?

एतन्मे संशयं कृष्ण छेत्तुमर्हस्यशेषतः ।

त्वदन्यः संशयस्यास्य छेत्ता न ह्युपपद्यते

॥ ६-३९॥

O Krishna, please dispel this doubt of mine completely, for who other than you can do so?

श्रीभगवानुवाच ।

पार्थ नैवेह नामुत्र विनाशस्तस्य विद्यते ।

न हि कल्याणकृत्कश्चिद् दुर्गतिं तात गच्छति

॥ ६-४०॥

The Supreme Lord said: O Parth, One who engages on the spiritual path does not meet with destruction either in this world or the world to come. My dear friend, one who strives for God-realization is never overcome by evil.

प्राप्य पुण्यकृतां लोकानुषित्वा शाश्वतीः समाः ।

शुचीनां श्रीमतां गेहे योगभ्रष्टोऽभिजायते

॥ ६-४१॥

अथवा योगिनामेव कुले भवति धीमताम् ।

एतद्धि दुर्लभतरं लोके जन्म यदीदृशम्

॥ ६-४२॥

The unsuccessful yogis, upon death, go to the abodes of the virtuous. After dwelling there for many ages, they are again reborn in the earth plane, into a family of pious and prosperous people. Else, if they had developed dispassion due to long practice of Yog, they are born into a family endowed with divine wisdom. Such a birth is very difficult to attain in this world.

तत्र तं बुद्धिसंयोगं लभते पौर्वदेहिकम् ।

यतते च ततो भूयः संसिद्धौ कुरुनन्दन

॥ ६-४३॥

On taking such a birth, O descendant of Kurus, they reawaken the wisdom of their previous lives, and strive even harder toward perfection in Yog.

karmī (ritualistic performer). Therefore, O Arjun, strive to be a yogi.

योगिनामपि सर्वेषां मद्गतेनान्तरात्मना ।
श्रद्धावान्भजते यो मां स मे युक्ततमो मतः

॥ ६-४७॥

Of all yogis, those whose minds are always absorbed in me, and who engage in devotion to me with great faith, them I consider to be the highest of all.

ॐ तत्सदिति श्रीमद्भगवद्गीतासूपनिषत्सु
ब्रह्मविद्यायां योगशास्त्रे श्रीकृष्णार्जुनसंवादे
आत्मसंयमयोगो नाम षष्ठोऽध्यायः

॥ ६॥

अथ सप्तमोऽध्यायः । ज्ञानविज्ञानयोगः

Beyond achievers of vast deeds! Be thou
Yogi Arjuna! And of such believe,
Truest and best is he who worships Me
With inmost soul, stayed on My Mystery!

HERE ENDETH CHAPTER VI. OF THE BHAGAVAD-GITA.

CHAPTER VII

This chapter begins by describing the material and spiritual dimensions of God's energies. Shree Krishna explains that all these have emanated from him, and they rest in him, as beads strung on a thread. He is the source of the entire creation, and into him it again dissolves. His material energy, Maya, is very difficult to overcome, but those who surrender to him receive his grace and cross over it easily.

Shree Krishna describes the four kinds of people who do not surrender to him, and the four kinds of people who engage in his devotion. Amongst his devotees, he considers as most dear, those who worship him in knowledge, with mind and intellect merged in him. Some, whose intellect has been carried away by material desires, surrender to the celestial gods. But these celestial gods can only bestow temporary material fruits, and even those, by the powers they have received from the Supreme Lord. Thus, the most worthy object of devotion is God himself.

श्रीभगवानुवाच ।

मय्यासक्तमनाः पार्थ योगं युञ्जन्मदाश्रयः ।

असंशयं समग्रं मां यथा ज्ञास्यसि तच्छृणु

॥ ७-१॥

The Supreme Lord said: Now listen, O Arjun, how, with the mind attached exclusively to me, and surrendering to me through the practice of bhakti yog, you can know me completely, free from doubt.

ज्ञानं तेऽहं सविज्ञानमिदं वक्ष्याम्यशेषतः ।

यज्ज्ञात्वा नेह भूयोऽन्यज्ज्ञातव्यमवशिष्यते

॥ ७-२॥

I shall now reveal unto you fully this knowledge and wisdom, knowing which nothing else remains to be known in this world.

मनुष्याणां सहस्रेषु कश्चिद्यतति सिद्धये ।
यततामपि सिद्धानां कश्चिन्मां वेत्ति तत्त्वतः

॥ ७-३॥

Amongst thousands of persons, hardly one strives for perfection; and amongst those who have achieved perfection, hardly one knows me in truth.

भूमिरापोऽनलो वायुः खं मनो बुद्धिरेव च ।
अहङ्कार इतीयं मे भिन्ना प्रकृतिरष्टधा

॥ ७-४॥

Earth, water, fire, air, space, mind, intellect, and ego—these are eight components of my material energy.

अपरेयमितस्त्वन्यां प्रकृतिं विद्धि मे पराम् ।
जीवभूतां महाबाहो ययेदं धार्यते जगत्

॥ ७-५॥

Such is my inferior energy. But beyond it, O mighty-armed Arjun, I have a superior energy. This is the jīva śhakti (the soul energy), which comprises the embodied souls who are the basis of life in this world.

एतद्योनीनि भूतानि सर्वाणीत्युपधारय ।
अहं कृत्स्नस्य जगतः प्रभवः प्रलयस्तथा
॥ ७-६॥

Know that all living beings are manifested by these two energies of mine. I am the source of the entire creation, and into me it again dissolves.

मत्तः परतरं नान्यत्किञ्चिदस्ति धनञ्जय ।
मयि सर्वमिदं प्रोतं सूत्रे मणिगणा इव
॥ ७-७॥

There is nothing higher than myself, O Arjun. Everything rests in me, as beads strung on a thread.

रसोऽहमप्सु कौन्तेय प्रभास्मि शशिसूर्ययोः ।
प्रणवः सर्ववेदेषु शब्दः खे पौरुषं नृषु
॥ ७-८॥

I am the taste in water, O son of Kunti, and the radiance of the sun and the moon. I am the sacred syllable Om in the Vedic mantras; I am the sound in ether, and the ability in humans.

पुण्यो गन्धः पृथिव्यां च तेजश्चास्मि विभावसौ ।

जीवनं सर्वभूतेषु तपश्चास्मि तपस्विषु

॥ ७- ९॥

I am the pure fragrance of the Earth, and the brilliance in fire. I am the life-force in all beings, and the penance of the ascetics.

बीजं मां सर्वभूतानां विद्धि पार्थ सनातनम् ।

बुद्धिर्बुद्धिमतामस्मि तेजस्तेजस्विनामहम्

॥ ७-१०॥

O Arjun, know that I am the eternal seed of all beings. I am the intellect of the intelligent, and the splendor of the glorious.

बलं बलवतां चाहं कामरागविवर्जितम् ।

धर्माविरुद्धो भूतेषु कामोऽस्मि भरतर्षभ

॥ ७-११॥

O best of the Bharatas, in strong persons, I am their strength devoid of desire and passion. I am sexual activity not conflicting with virtue or scriptural injunctions.

ये चैव सात्त्विका भावा राजसास्तामसाश्च ये ।

मत्त एवेति तान्विद्धि न त्वहं तेषु ते मयि

॥ ७-१२॥

The three states of material existence—goodness, passion, and ignorance—are manifested by my energy. They are in me, but I am beyond them.

त्रिभिर्गुणमयैर्भावैरेभिः सर्वमिदं जगत् ।

मोहितं नाभिजानाति मामेभ्यः परमव्ययम्

॥ ७-१३॥

Deluded by the three modes of Maya, the people in this world are unable to know me, the imperishable and eternal.

दैवी ह्येषा गुणमयी मम माया दुरत्यया ।

मामेव ये प्रपद्यन्ते मायामेतां तरन्ति ते

॥ ७-१४॥

My divine energy Maya, consisting of the three modes of nature, is very difficult to overcome. But those who surrender unto me cross over it easily.

न मां दुष्कृतिनो मूढाः प्रपद्यन्ते नराधमाः ।

माययापहृतज्ञाना आसुरं भावमाश्रिताः

॥ ७-१५॥

Four kinds of people do not surrender unto me—those ignorant of knowledge, those who lazily follow their lower nature though capable of knowing me, those with deluded intellect, and those with a demoniac nature.

चतुर्विधा भजन्ते मां जनाः सुकृतिनोऽर्जुन ।

आर्तो जिज्ञासुरर्थार्थी ज्ञानी च भरतर्षभ

॥ ७-१६॥

O best amongst the Bharatas, four kinds of pious people engage in my devotion—the distressed, the seekers after knowledge, the seekers of worldly possessions, and those who are situated in knowledge.

तेषां ज्ञानी नित्ययुक्त एकभक्तिर्विशिष्यते ।

प्रियो हि ज्ञानिनोऽत्यर्थमहं स च मम प्रियः

॥ ७-१७॥

Amongst these, I consider them to be the highest, who worship me with knowledge, and are steadfastly and exclusively devoted to me. I am very dear to them and they are dear to me.

उदाराः सर्व एवैते ज्ञानी त्वात्मैव मे मतम् ।

आस्थितः स हि युक्तात्मा मामेवानुत्तमां गतिम्

॥ ७-१८॥

Indeed, all those who are devoted to me are indeed noble. But those in knowledge, who are of steadfast mind, whose intellect is merged in me, and who have made me alone as their supreme goal, I consider as my very self.

बहूनां जन्मनामन्ते ज्ञानवान्मां प्रपद्यते ।

वासुदेवः सर्वमिति स महात्मा सुदुर्लभः

॥ ७-१९॥

After many births of spiritual practice, one who is endowed with knowledge surrenders unto me, knowing me to be all that is. Such a great soul is indeed very rare.

कामैस्तैस्तैर्हृतज्ञानाः प्रपद्यन्तेऽन्यदेवताः ।

तं तं नियममास्थाय प्रकृत्या नियताः स्वया

॥ ७-२०॥

Those whose knowledge has been carried away by material desires surrender to the celestial gods. Following their own nature, they worship the devatās, practicing rituals meant to propitiate these celestial personalities.

यो यो यां यां तनुं भक्तः श्रद्धयार्चितुमिच्छति ।

तस्य तस्याचलां श्रद्धां तामेव विदधाम्यहम्

॥ ७-२१॥

Whatever celestial form, devotee seeks to worship with faith, I steady the faith of such devotee in that form.

स तया श्रद्धया युक्तस्तस्याराधनमीहते ।

लभते च ततः कामान्मयैव विहितान्हि तान्

॥ ७-२२॥

Endowed with faith, the devotee worships a particular celestial god and obtains the objects of desire. But in reality I alone arrange these benefits.

अन्तवत्तु फलं तेषां तद्भवत्यल्पमेधसाम् ।

देवान्देवयजो यान्ति मद्भक्ता यान्ति मामपि

॥ ७-२३॥

But the fruit gained by these people of small understanding is perishable. Those who worship the celestial gods go to the celestial abodes, while my devotees come to me.

अव्यक्तं व्यक्तिमापन्नं मन्यन्ते मामबुद्धयः ।

परं भावमजानन्तो ममाव्ययमनुत्तमम्

॥ ७-२४॥

The less intelligent think that I, the Supreme Lord Shree Krishna, was formless earlier and have now assumed this personality. They do not understand the imperishable exalted nature of my personal form.

नाहं प्रकाशः सर्वस्य योगमायासमावृतः ।

मूढोऽयं नाभिजानाति लोको मामजमव्ययम्

॥ ७-२५॥

I am not manifest to everyone, being veiled by my divine Yogmaya energy. Hence, those without knowledge do not know that I am without birth and changeless.

वेदाहं समतीतानि वर्तमानानि चार्जुन ।

भविष्याणि च भूतानि मां तु वेद न कश्चन

॥ ७-२६॥

O Arjun, I know of the the past, present, and future, and I also know all living beings; but me no one knows.

इच्छाद्वेषसमुत्थेन द्वन्द्वमोहेन भारत ।

सर्वभूतानि सम्मोहं सर्गे यान्ति परन्तप

॥ ७-२७॥

O descendant of Bharat, the dualities of desire and aversion arise from illusion. O conqueror of enemies, all living beings in the material realm are from birth deluded by these.

अथ अष्टमोऽध्यायः ।   अक्षरब्रह्मयोगः

Know I am ADHIBHUTA, Lord of Life,
And ADHIDAIVA, Lord of all the Gods,
And ADHIYAJNA, Lord of Sacrifice;
Worship Me well, with hearts of love and faith,

And find and hold me in the hour of death.

HERE ENDETH CHAPTER VII OF THE BHAGAVAD-GITA.

CHAPTER VIII

अर्जुन उवाच ।

किं तद् ब्रह्म किमध्यात्मं किं कर्म पुरुषोत्तम ।
अधिभूतं च किं प्रोक्तमधिदैवं किमुच्यते
॥ ८-१॥

अधियज्ञः कथं कोऽत्र देहेऽस्मिन्मधुसूदन ।
प्रयाणकाले च कथं ज्ञेयोऽसि नियतात्मभिः
॥ ८-२॥

Arjun said: O Supreme Lord, what is Brahman (Absolute Reality), what is adhyātma (the individual soul), and what is karma? What is said to be adhibhūta, and who is said to be Adhidaiva? Who is Adhiyajña in the body and how is He the Adhiyajña? O Krishna, how are You to be known at the time of death by those of steadfast mind?

श्रीभगवानुवाच ।

अक्षरं ब्रह्म परमं स्वभावोऽध्यात्ममुच्यते ।

भूतभावोद्भवकरो विसर्गः कर्मसंज्ञितः

॥ ८-३॥

The Blessed Lord said: The Supreme Indestructible Entity is called Brahman; one's own self is called adhyātma. Actions pertaining to the material personality of living beings, and its development are called karma, or fruitive activities.

अधिभूतं क्षरो भावः पुरुषश्चाधिदैवतम् ।

अधियज्ञोऽहमेवात्र देहे देहभृतां वर

॥ ८-४॥

O best of the embodied souls, the physical manifestation that is constantly changing is called adhibhūta; the universal form of God, which presides over the celestial gods in this creation, is called adhidaiva; I, who dwell in the heart of every living being, am called Adhiyajña, or the Lord of all sacrifices.

अन्तकाले च मामेव स्मरन्मुक्त्वा कलेवरम् ।

यः प्रयाति स मद्भावं याति नास्त्यत्र संशयः

॥ ८-५॥

Those who relinquish the body while remembering Me at the moment of death will come to Me. There is certainly no doubt about this.

यं यं वापि स्मरन्भावं त्यजत्यन्ते कलेवरम् ।

तं तमेवैति कौन्तेय सदा तद्भावभावितः

॥ ८-६॥

Whatever one remembers upon giving up the body at the time of death, O son of Kunti, one attains that state, being always absorbed in such contemplation.

तस्मात्सर्वेषु कालेषु मामनुस्मर युध्य च ।

मय्यर्पितमनोबुद्धिर्मामेवैष्यस्यसंशयः

॥ ८-७॥

Therefore, always remember Me and also do your duty of fighting the war. With mind and intellect surrendered to Me, you will definitely attain Me; of this, there is no doubt.

अभ्यासयोगयुक्तेन चेतसा नान्यगामिना ।

परमं पुरुषं दिव्यं याति पार्थानुचिन्तयन्

॥ ८-८॥

With practice, O Parth, when you constantly engage the mind in remembering Me, the Supreme Divine Personality, without deviating, you will certainly attain Me.

कविं पुराणमनुशासितार-

मणोरणीयंसमनुस्मरेद्यः ।

सर्वस्य धातारमचिन्त्यरूप-

मादित्यवर्णं तमसः परस्तात्

॥ ८-९॥

प्रयाणकाले मनसाऽचलेन

भक्त्या युक्तो योगबलेन चैव ।

भ्रुवोर्मध्ये प्राणमावेश्य सम्यक्

स तं परं पुरुषमुपैति दिव्यम्

॥ ८-१०॥

God is Omniscient, the most ancient one, the Controller, subtler than the subtlest, the Support of all, and the possessor of an inconceivable divine form; He is brighter than the sun, and beyond all darkness of ignorance. One who at the time of death, with unmoving mind attained by the practice of Yog, fixes the prāṇ (life airs) between the eyebrows, and steadily remembers the Divine Lord with great devotion, certainly attains Him.

यदक्षरं वेदविदो वदन्ति

विशन्ति यद्यतयो वीतरागाः ।

यदिच्छन्तो ब्रह्मचर्यं चरन्ति

तत्ते पदं सङ्ग्रहेण प्रवक्ष्ये

॥ ८-११॥

Scholars of the Vedas describe Him as Imperishable; great ascetics practice the vow of celibacy and renounce worldly pleasures to enter into Him. I shall now explain to you briefly the path to that goal.

सर्वद्वाराणि संयम्य मनो हृदि निरुध्य च ।

मूर्ध्न्याधायात्मनः प्राणमास्थितो योगधारणाम्

॥ ८-१२॥

Restraining all the gates of the body and fixing the mind in the heart region, and then drawing the life-breath to the head, one should get established in steadfast yogic concentration.

मामुपेत्य पुनर्जन्म दुःखालयमशाश्वतम् ।

नाप्नुवन्ति महात्मानः संसिद्धिं परमां गताः

॥ ८-१५॥

Having attained Me, the great souls are no more subject to rebirth in this world, which is transient and full of misery, because they have attained the highest perfection.

आब्रह्मभुवनाल्लोकाः पुनरावर्तिनोऽर्जुन ।

मामुपेत्य तु कौन्तेय पुनर्जन्म न विद्यते

॥ ८-१६॥

In all the worlds of this material creation, up to the highest abode of Brahma, you will be subject to rebirth, O Arjun. But on attaining My Abode, O son of Kunti, there is no further rebirth.

ओमित्येकाक्षरं ब्रह्म व्याहरन्मामनुस्मरन् ।
यः प्रयाति त्यजन्देहं स याति परमां गतिम्

॥ ८-१३॥

highest abode of Brahma, you will be subject to rebirth, O Arjun. But on attaining My Abode, O son of Kunti, there is no further rebirth.

One who departs from the body while remembering Me, the Supreme Personality, and chanting the syllable Om, will attain the supreme goal.

अनन्यचेताः सततं यो मां स्मरति नित्यशः ।
तस्याहं सुलभः पार्थ नित्ययुक्तस्य योगिनः

॥ ८-१४॥

O Parth, for those yogis who always think of Me with exclusive devotion, I am easily attainable because of their constant absorption in Me.

सहस्रयुगपर्यन्तमहर्यद् ब्रह्मणो विदुः ।

रात्रिं युगसहस्रान्तां तेऽहोरात्रविदो जनाः

॥ ८-१७॥

One day of Brahma (kalp) lasts a thousand cycles of the four ages (mahā yug) and his night also extends for the same span of time. The wise who know this understand the reality about day and night.

अव्यक्ताद् व्यक्तयः सर्वाः प्रभवन्त्यहरागमे ।

रात्र्यागमे प्रलीयन्ते तत्रैवाव्यक्तसंज्ञके

॥ ८-१८॥

At the advent of Brahma's day, all living beings emanate from the unmanifest source. And at the fall of his night, all embodied beings again merge into their unmanifest source.

भूतग्रामः स एवायं भूत्वा भूत्वा प्रलीयते ।

रात्र्यागमेऽवशः पार्थ प्रभवत्यहरागमे

॥ ८-१९॥

The multitudes of beings repeatedly take birth with the advent of Brahma's day, and are reabsorbed on the arrival of the cosmic night, to manifest again automatically on the advent of the next cosmic day.

परस्तस्मात्तु भावोऽन्योऽव्यक्तोऽव्यक्तात्सनातनः ।

यः स सर्वेषु भूतेषु नश्यत्सु न विनश्यति

॥ ८-२०॥

Transcendental to this manifest and unmanifest creation, there is yet another unmanifest eternal dimension. That realm does not cease even when all others do.

अव्यक्तोऽक्षर इत्युक्तस्तमाहुः परमां गतिम् ।

यं प्राप्य न निवर्तन्ते तद्धाम परमं मम

॥ ८-२१॥

That unmanifest dimension is the supreme goal, and upon reaching it, one never returns to this mortal world. That is My supreme Abode.

धूमो रात्रिस्तथा कृष्णः षण्मासा दक्षिणायनम् ।
तत्र चान्द्रमसं ज्योतिर्योगी प्राप्य निवर्तते
॥ ८-२२ - ८-२५॥

The Supreme Divine Personality is greater than all that exists. Although He is all-pervading and all living beings are situated in Him, yet He can be known only through devotion.

शुक्लकृष्णे गती ह्येते जगतः शाश्वते मते ।
एकया यात्यनावृत्तिमन्ययावर्तते पुनः
॥ ८-२६॥

I shall now describe to you the different paths of passing away from this world, O best of the Bharatas, one of which leads to liberation and the other leads to rebirth. Those who know the Supreme Brahman, and who depart from this world, during the six months of the sun's northern course, the bright fortnight of the moon, and the bright part of the day, attain the supreme destination. The practitioners of Vedic rituals, who pass away during the six months of the sun's southern course, the dark fortnight of the moon, the time of smoke, the night, attain the celestial abodes. After enjoying celestial pleasures, they again return to the earth. These two, bright and dark paths, always exist in this world. The way of light leads to liberation and the way of darkness leads to rebirth.

नैते सृती पार्थ जानन्योगी मुह्यति कश्चन ।

तस्मात्सर्वेषु कालेषु योगयुक्तो भवार्जुन

॥ ८-२७॥

Yogis who know the secret of these two paths, O Parth, are never bewildered. Therefore, at all times be situated in Yog (union with God).

अग्निर्ज्योतिरहः शुक्लः षण्मासा उत्तरायणम् ।

तत्र प्रयाता गच्छन्ति ब्रह्म ब्रह्मविदो जनाः

॥ ८-२४॥

Yogis who know the secret of these two paths, O Parth, are never bewildered. Therefore, at all times be situated in Yog (union with God).

वेदेषु यज्ञेषु तपःसु चैव

दानेषु यत्पुण्यफलं प्रदिष्टम् ।

अत्येति तत्सर्वमिदं विदित्वा

योगी परं स्थानमुपैति चाद्यम्

॥ ८-२८॥

The yogis, who know this secret, gain merit far beyond the fruits of Vedic rituals, the study of the Vedas, performance of sacrifices, austerities, and charities. Such yogis reach the Supreme Abode.

ॐ तत्सदिति श्रीमद्भगवद्गीतासूपनिषत्सु

ब्रह्मविद्यायां योगशास्त्रे श्रीकृष्णार्जुनसंवादे

अक्षरब्रह्मयोगो नामाष्टमोऽध्यायः

॥ ८॥

अथ नवमोऽध्यायः । राजविद्याराजगुह्ययोगः

Richer than holy fruit on Vedas growing,
Greater than gifts, better than prayer or fast,
Such wisdom is! The Yogi, this way knowing,

Comes to the Utmost Perfect Peace at last.

HERE ENDETH CHAPTER VIII. OF THE BHAGAVAD-GITA.

CHAPTER IX

श्रीभगवानुवाच ।

इदं तु ते गुह्यतमं प्रवक्ष्याम्यनसूयवे ।

ज्ञानं विज्ञानसहितं यज्ज्ञात्वा मोक्ष्यसेऽशुभात्

॥ ९-१ ॥

The Supreme Lord said: O Arjun, because you are not envious of Me, I shall now impart to you this very confidential knowledge and wisdom, upon knowing which you will be released from the miseries of material existence.

राजविद्या राजगुह्यं पवित्रमिदमुत्तमम् ।

प्रत्यक्षावगमं धर्म्यं सुसुखं कर्तुमव्ययम्

॥ ९-२ ॥

This knowledge is the king of sciences and the most profound of all secrets. It purifies those who hear it. It is directly realizable, in accordance with dharma, easy to practice, and everlasting in effect.

अश्रद्दधानाः पुरुषा धर्मस्यास्य परन्तप ।

अप्राप्य मां निवर्तन्ते मृत्युसंसारवर्त्मनि

॥ ९-३॥

People who have no faith in this dharma are unable to attain Me, O conqueror of enemies. They repeatedly come back to this world in the cycle of birth and death.

मया ततमिदं सर्वं जगदव्यक्तमूर्तिना ।

मत्स्थानि सर्वभूतानि न चाहं तेष्ववस्थितः

॥ ९-४॥

This entire cosmic manifestation is pervaded by Me in My unmanifest form. All living beings dwell in Me, but I do not dwell in them.

न च मत्स्थानि भूतानि पश्य मे योगमैश्वरम् ।

भूतभृन्न च भूतस्थो ममात्मा भूतभावनः

॥ ९-५॥

And yet, the living beings do not abide in Me. Behold the mystery of My divine energy! Although I am the Creator and Sustainer of all living beings, I am not influenced by them or by material nature.

यथाकाशस्थितो नित्यं वायुः सर्वत्रगो महान् ।

तथा सर्वाणि भूतानि मत्स्थानीत्युपधारय

॥ ९-६॥

Know that as the mighty wind blowing everywhere rests always in the sky, likewise all living beings rest always in Me.

सर्वभूतानि कौन्तेय प्रकृतिं यान्ति मामिकाम् ।

कल्पक्षये पुनस्तानि कल्पादौ विसृजाम्यहम्

॥ ९-७॥

O son of Kunti, at the end of the millennium every material manifestation enters into My nature, and at the beginning of another millennium, by My potency I again create.

प्रकृतिं स्वामवष्टभ्य विसृजामि पुनः पुनः ।

भूतग्राममिमं कृत्स्नमवशं प्रकृतेर्वशात्

॥ ९-८॥

The whole cosmic order is under Me. By My will it is manifested again and again, and by My will it is annihilated at the end.

न च मां तानि कर्माणि निबध्नन्ति धनञ्जय ।

उदासीनवदासीनमसक्तं तेषु कर्मसु

॥ ९-९॥

O Dhananjaya, all this work cannot bind Me. I am ever detached, seated as though neutral.

मयाध्यक्षेण प्रकृतिः सूयते सचराचरम् ।

हेतुनानेन कौन्तेय जगद्विपरिवर्तते

॥ ९-१०॥

Working under My direction, this material energy brings into being all animate and inanimate forms, O son of Kunti. For this reason, the material world undergoes the changes (of creation, maintenance, and dissolution).

अवजानन्ति मां मूढा मानुषीं तनुमाश्रितम् ।

परं भावमजानन्तो मम भूतमहेश्वरम्

॥ ९-११॥

When I descend in My personal form deluded persons are unable to recognize Me. They do not know the divinity of My personality, as the Supreme Lord of all beings.

मोघाशा मोघकर्माणो मोघज्ञाना विचेतसः ।
राक्षसीमासुरीं चैव प्रकृतिं मोहिनीं श्रिताः

॥ ९-१२॥

Bewildered by the material energy, such persons embrace demoniac and atheistic views. In that deluded state, their hopes for welfare are in vain, their fruitive actions are wasted, and their culture of knowledge is baffled.

महात्मानस्तु मां पार्थ दैवीं प्रकृतिमाश्रिताः ।
भजन्त्यनन्यमनसो ज्ञात्वा भूतादिमव्ययम्

॥ ९-१३॥

But the great souls, who take shelter of My divine energy, O Parth, know Me, Lord Krishna, as the origin of all creation. They engage in My devotion with their minds fixed exclusively on Me.

सततं कीर्तयन्तो मां यतन्तश्च दृढव्रताः ।
नमस्यन्तश्च मां भक्त्या नित्ययुक्ता उपासते

॥ ९-१४॥

Always singing My divine glories, striving with great determination, and humbly bowing down before Me, they constantly worship Me in loving devotion.

ज्ञानयज्ञेन चाप्यन्ये यजन्तो मामुपासते ।

एकत्वेन पृथक्त्वेन बहुधा विश्वतोमुखम्

॥ ९-१५॥

Others, engaging in the yajña of cultivating knowledge, worship Me by many methods. Some see Me as undifferentiated oneness that is non-different from them, while others see Me as separate from them. Still others worship Me in the infinite manifestations of My cosmic form.

अहं क्रतुरहं यज्ञः स्वधाहमहमौषधम् ।

मन्त्रोऽहमहमेवाज्यमहमग्निरहं हुतम्

॥ ९-१६॥

But it is I who am the ritual, I the sacrifice, the offering to the ancestors, the healing herb, the transcendental chant. I am the butter and the fire and the offering.

पिताहमस्य जगतो माता धाता पितामहः ।

वेद्यं पवित्रमोङ्कार ऋक्साम यजुरेव च

॥ ९-१७॥

I am the father of this universe, the mother, the support, and the grandsire. I am the object of knowledge, the purifier and the syllable om. I am also the Rk, the Sama, and the Yajur [Vedas].

गतिर्भर्ता प्रभुः साक्षी निवासः शरणं सुहृत् ।
प्रभवः प्रलयः स्थानं निधानं बीजमव्ययम्
॥ ९-१८॥

I am the goal, the sustainer, the master, the witness, the abode, the refuge and the most dear friend. I am the creation and the annihilation, the basis of everything, the resting place and the eternal seed.

तपाम्यहमहं वर्षं निगृह्णाम्युत्सृजामि च ।
अमृतं चैव मृत्युश्च सदसच्चाहमर्जुन
॥ ९-१९॥

O Arjuna, I control heat, the rain and the drought. I am immortality, and I am also death personified. Both being and nonbeing are in Me.

त्रैविद्या मां सोमपाः पूतपापा
यज्ञैरिष्ट्वा स्वर्गतिं प्रार्थयन्ते ।
ते पुण्यमासाद्य सुरेन्द्रलोक-
मश्नन्ति दिव्यान्दिवि देवभोगान् ॥ ९-२०॥

Those who study the Vedas and drink the soma juice, seeking the heavenly planets, worship Me indirectly. They take birth on the planet of Indra, where they enjoy godly delights.

ते तं भुक्त्वा स्वर्गलोकं विशालं

क्षीणे पुण्ये मर्त्यलोकं विशन्ति ।

एवं त्रयीधर्ममनुप्रपन्ना

गतागतं कामकामा लभन्ते

॥ ९-२१॥

When they have thus enjoyed heavenly sense pleasure, they return to this mortal planet again. Thus, through the Vedic principles, they achieve only flickering happiness.

अनन्याश्चिन्तयन्तो मां ये जनाः पर्युपासते ।

तेषां नित्याभियुक्तानां योगक्षेमं वहाम्यहम्

॥ ९-२२॥

But those who worship Me with devotion, meditating on My transcendental form-to them I carry what they lack and preserve what they have.

येऽप्यन्यदेवता भक्ता यजन्ते श्रद्धयान्विताः ।

तेऽपि मामेव कौन्तेय यजन्त्यविधिपूर्वकम्

॥ ९-२३॥

Whatever a man may sacrifice to other gods, O son of Kunti, is really meant for Me alone, but it is offered without true understanding.

अहं हि सर्वयज्ञानां भोक्ता च प्रभुरेव च ।

न तु मामभिजानन्ति तत्त्वेनातश्च्यवन्ति ते

॥ ९-२४॥

I am the only enjoyer and the only object of sacrifice. Those who do not recognize My true transcendental nature fall down.

यान्ति देवव्रता देवान्पितृन्यान्ति पितृव्रताः ।

भूतानि यान्ति भूतेज्या यान्ति मद्याजिनोऽपि माम्

॥ ९-२५॥

Those who worship the demigods will take birth among the demigods; those who worship ghosts and spirits will take birth among such beings; those who worship ancestors go to the ancestors; and those who worship Me will live with Me.

पत्रं पुष्पं फलं तोयं यो मे भक्त्या प्रयच्छति ।

तदहं भक्त्युपहृतमश्नामि प्रयतात्मनः

॥ ९-२६॥

If one offers Me with love and devotion a leaf, a flower, fruit a water, I will accept it.

यत्करोषि यदश्नासि यज्जुहोषि ददासि यत् ।

यत्तपस्यसि कौन्तेय तत्कुरुष्व मदर्पणम्

॥ ९-२७॥

O son of Kunti, all that you do, all that you eat, all that you offer and give away, as well as all austerities that you may perform, should be done as an offering unto Me.

शुभाशुभफलैरेवं मोक्ष्यसे कर्मबन्धनैः ।
संन्यासयोगयुक्तात्मा विमुक्तो मामुपैष्यसि

॥ ९-२८॥

In this way you will be freed from all reactions to good and evil deeds, and by this principle of renunciation you will be liberated and come to Me.

समोऽहं सर्वभूतेषु न मे द्वेष्योऽस्ति न प्रियः ।
ये भजन्ति तु मां भक्त्या मयि ते तेषु चाप्यहम्

॥ ९-२९॥

I envy no one, nor am I partial to anyone. I am equal to all. But whoever renders service unto Me in devotion is a friend, is in Me, and I am also a friend to him.

अपि चेत्सुदुराचारो भजते मामनन्यभाक् ।
साधुरेव स मन्तव्यः सम्यग्व्यवसितो हि सः

॥ ९-३०॥

Even if one commits the most abominable actions, if he is engaged in devotional service, he is to be considered saintly because he is properly situated.

क्षिप्रं भवति धर्मात्मा शश्वच्छान्तिं निगच्छति ।

कौन्तेय प्रतिजानीहि न मे भक्तः प्रणश्यति

॥ ९-३१ ॥

He quickly becomes righteous and attains lasting peace. O son of Kunti, declare it boldly that My devotee never perishes.

मां हि पार्थ व्यपाश्रित्य येऽपि स्युः पापयोनयः ।

स्त्रियो वैश्यास्तथा शूद्रास्तेऽपि यान्ति परां गतिम्

॥ ९-३२ ॥

O son of Prtha, those who take shelter in Me, though they be of lower birth-women, vaisyas [merchants], as well as sudras [workers]-can approach the supreme destination.

किं पुनर्ब्राह्मणाः पुण्या भक्ता राजर्षयस्तथा ।

अनित्यमसुखं लोकमिमं प्राप्य भजस्व माम्

॥ ९-३३ ॥

How much greater then are the brahmanas, the righteous, the devotees and saintly kings who in this temporary miserable world engage in loving service unto Me.

मन्मना भव मद्भक्तो मद्याजी मां नमस्कुरु ।
मामेवैष्यसि युक्त्वैवमात्मानं मत्परायणः
॥ ९-३४॥

Engage your mind always in thinking of Me, offer obeisances and worship Me. Being completely absorbed in Me, surely you will come to Me.

ॐ तत्सदिति श्रीमद्भगवद्गीतासूपनिषत्सु
ब्रह्मविद्यायां योगशास्त्रे श्रीकृष्णार्जुनसंवादे
राजविद्याराजगुह्ययोगो नाम नवमोऽध्यायः ॥ ९॥

अथ दशमोऽध्यायः । विभूतियोगः

Ah! Ye who into this ill world are come--
Fleeting and false--set your faith fast on Me!
Fix heart and thought on Me! Adore Me! Bring
Offerings to Me! Make Me prostrations! Make
Me your supremest joy! And, undivided,
Unto My rest your spirits shall be guided.

HERE ENDS CHAPTER IX OF THE BHAGAVAD-GITA.

CHAPTER X

This chapter is narrated by Lord Krishna to help Arjun meditate on God by reflecting upon his magnificent and resplendent glories. In chapter nine, Shree Krishna revealed the science of bhakti, or loving devotion, and described some of his opulences. Here, he expounds further on his infinite glories, with the desire to increase Arjun's bhakti. These verses are pleasing to read and enchanting to hear.

Shree Krishna reveals that he is the source of everything that exists. The varieties of qualities of humans arise from him. The seven great Sages, the four great Saints, and the fourteen Manus were born from his mind, and from them all people in the world have descended. Those who know that everything proceeds from him engage in his devotion with great faith. Such devotees derive great satisfaction in conversing about his glories and enlightening others about him. Since their minds are united with him, he dwelling within their hearts gives the divine knowledge by which they can easily attain him.

श्रीभगवानुवाच ।

भूय एव महाबाहो शृणु मे परमं वचः ।

यत्तेऽहं प्रीयमाणाय वक्ष्यामि हितकाम्यया

॥ १०-१॥

The Blessed Lord said: Listen again to my divine teachings, O mighty armed one. Desiring your welfare because you are my beloved friend, I shall reveal them to you.

न मे विदुः सुरगणाः प्रभवं न महर्षयः ।

अहमादिर्हि देवानां महर्षीणां च सर्वशः

॥ १०-२॥

Neither celestial gods nor the great sages know my origin. I am the source from which the gods and great seers come.

यो मामजमनादिं च वेत्ति लोकमहेश्वरम् ।

असम्मूढः स मर्त्येषु सर्वपापैः प्रमुच्यते

॥ १०-३॥

Those who know me as unborn and beginningless, and as the Supreme Lord of the universe, they among mortals are free from illusion and released from all evils.

बुद्धिर्ज्ञानमसम्मोहः क्षमा सत्यं दमः शमः ।

सुखं दुःखं भवोऽभावो भयं चाभयमेव च ॥ १०-४॥

अहिंसा समता तुष्टिस्तपो दानं यशोऽयशः ।

भवन्ति भावा भूतानां मत्त एव पृथग्विधाः

॥ १०-५॥

Intelligence, knowledge, freedom from doubt and delusion, forgiveness, truthfulness, self-control and calmness, pleasure and pain, birth, death, fear, fearlessness, nonviolence, equanimity, satisfaction, austerity, charity, fame and infamy are created by Me alone.

महर्षयः सप्त पूर्वे चत्वारो मनवस्तथा ।

मद्भावा मानसा जाता येषां लोक इमाः प्रजाः

॥ १०-६॥

The seven great sages and before them the four other great sages and the Manus [progenitors of mankind] are born out of My mind, and all creatures in these planets descend from them.

एतां विभूतिं योगं च मम यो वेत्ति तत्त्वतः ।

सोऽविकम्पेन योगेन युज्यते नात्र संशयः

॥ १०-७॥

He who knows in truth this glory and power of Mine engages in unalloyed devotional service; of this there is no doubt.

अहं सर्‌वस्‌य प्‌रभवो मत्‌तः सर्‌वं प्‌रवर्‌तते ।

इति मत्वा भजन्ते मां बुधा भावसमन्विताः

॥ १०-८॥

I am the origin of all creation. Everything proceeds from me. The wise who know this perfectly worship me with great faith and devotion.

मच्चित्ता मद्गतप्राणा बोधयन्तः परस्परम् ।
कथयन्तश्च मां नित्यं तुष्यन्ति च रमन्ति च

॥ १०-९॥

With their minds fixed on me and their lives surrendered to me, my devotees remain ever contented in me. They derive great satisfaction and bliss in enlightening one another about me, and conversing about my glories.

तेषां सततयुक्तानां भजतां प्रीतिपूर्वकम् ।
ददामि बुद्धियोगं तं येन मामुपयान्ति ते

॥ १०-१०॥

To those whose minds are always united with me in loving devotion, I give the divine knowledge by which they can attain me.

तेषामेवानुकम्पार्थमहमज्ञानजं तमः ।
नाशयाम्यात्मभावस्थो ज्ञानदीपेन भास्वता

॥ १०-११॥

Out of compassion for them, I, who dwell within their hearts, destroy the darkness born of ignorance, with the luminous lamp of knowledge.

अर्जुन उवाच ।

परं ब्रह्म परं धाम पवित्रं परमं भवान् ।
पुरुषं शाश्वतं दिव्यमादिदेवमजं विभुम्
॥ १०-१२॥

आहुस्त्वामृषयः सर्वे देवर्षिर्नारदस्तथा ।
असितो देवलो व्यासः स्वयं चैव ब्रवीषि मे
॥ १०-१३॥

Arjun said: You are the Supreme Divine Personality, the Supreme Abode, the Supreme Purifier, the Eternal God, the Primal Being, the Unborn, and the Greatest. The great sages, like Narad, Asit, Deval, and Vyas, proclaimed this, and now you are declaring it to me yourself.

सर्वमेतदृतं मन्ये यन्मां वदसि केशव ।
न हि ते भगवन्व्यक्तिं विदुर्देवा न दानवाः
॥ १०-१४॥

O Krishna, I totally accept everything you have told me as the truth. O Lord, neither gods nor the demons can understand your true personality.

स्वयमेवात्मनात्मानं वेत्थ त्वं पुरुषोत्तम ।

भूतभावन भूतेश देवदेव जगत्पते

॥ १०-१५॥

Indeed, you alone know yourself by your inconceivable energy, O Supreme Personality, the Creator and Lord of all beings, the God of gods, and the Lord of the universe!

वक्तुमर्हस्यशेषेण दिव्या ह्यात्मविभूतयः ।

याभिर्विभूतिभिर्लोकानिमांस्त्वं व्याप्य तिष्ठसि

॥ १०-१६॥

कथं विद्यामहं योगिंस्त्वां सदा परिचिन्तयन् ।

केषु केषु च भावेषु चिन्त्योऽसि भगवन्मया

॥ १०-१७॥

Please describe to me your divine opulences, by which you pervade all the worlds and reside in them. O Supreme Master of Yog, how may I know you and think of you. And while meditating, in what forms can I think of you, O Supreme Divine Personality?

विस्तरेणात्मनो योगं विभूतिं च जनार्दन ।

भूयः कथय तृप्तिर्हि शृण्वतो नास्ति मेऽमृतम्

॥ १०-१८॥

Tell me again in detail your divine glories and manifestations, O Janardan. I can never tire of hearing your nectar.

श्रीभगवानुवाच ।

हन्त ते कथयिष्यामि दिव्या ह्यात्मविभूतयः ।

प्राधान्यतः कुरुश्रेष्ठ नास्त्यन्तो विस्तरस्य मे

॥ १०-१९॥

The Blessed Lord spoke: I shall now briefly describe my divine glories to you, O best of the Kurus, for there is no end to their detail.

अहमात्मा गुडाकेश सर्वभूताशयस्थितः ।

अहमादिश्च मध्यं च भूतानामन्त एव च

॥ १०-२०॥

I am the Self, O Gudakesa, seated in the hearts of all creatures. I am the beginning, the middle and the end of all beings.

आदित्यानामहं विष्णुर्ज्योतिषां रविरंशुमान् ।
मरीचिर्मरुतामस्मि नक्षत्राणामहं शशी

॥ १०-२१॥

Of the Adityas I am Visnu, of lights I am the radiant sun, I am Marici of the Maruts, and among the stars I am the moon.

वेदानां सामवेदोऽस्मि देवानामस्मि वासवः ।
इन्द्रियाणां मनश्चास्मि भूतानामस्मि चेतना

॥ १०-२२॥

Of the Vedas I am the Sama-veda; of the demigods I am Indra; of the senses I am the mind, and in living beings I am the living force [knowledge].

रुद्राणां शङ्करश्चास्मि वित्तेशो यक्षरक्षसाम् ।
वसूनां पावकश्चास्मि मेरुः शिखरिणामहम्

॥ १०-२३॥

Of all the Rudras I am Lord Siva; of the Yaksas and Raksasas I am the lord of wealth [Kuvera]; of the Vasus I am fire [Agni], and of the mountains I am Meru.

पुरोधसां च मुख्यं मां विद्धि पार्थ बृहस्पतिम् ।
सेनानीनामहं स्कन्दः सरसामस्मि सागरः
॥ १०-२४॥

Of priests, O Arjuna, know Me to be the chief, Brhaspati, the lord of devotion. Of generals I am Skanda, the lord of war; and of bodies of water I am the ocean.

महर्षीणां भृगुरहं गिरामस्म्येकमक्षरम् ।
यज्ञानां जपयज्ञोऽस्मि स्थावराणां हिमालयः
॥ १०-२५॥

Of the great sages I am Bhrgu; of vibrations I am the transcendental om. Of sacrifices I am the chanting of the holy names [japa], and of immovable things I am the Himalayas.

अश्वत्थः सर्ववृक्षाणां देवर्षीणां च नारदः ।
गन्धर्वाणां चित्ररथः सिद्धानां कपिलो मुनिः
॥ १०-२६॥

Of all trees I am the holy fig tree, and amongst sages and demigods I am Narada. Of the singers of the gods [Gandharvas] I am Citraratha, and among perfected beings I am the sage Kapila.

उच्चैःश्रवसमश्वानां विद्धि माममृतोद्भवम् ।

ऐरावतं गजेन्द्राणां नराणां च नराधिपम्

॥ १०-२७॥

Of horses know Me to be Uccaihsrava, who rose out of the ocean, born of the elixir of immortality; of lordly elephants I am Airavata, and among men I am the monarch.

आयुधानामहं वज्रं धेनूनामस्मि कामधुक् ।

प्रजनश्चास्मि कन्दर्पः सर्पाणामस्मि वासुकिः

॥ १०-२८॥

Of weapons I am the thunderbolt; among cows I am the surabhi, givers of abundant milk. Of procreators I am Kandarpa, the god of love, and of serpents I am Vasuki, the chief.

अनन्तश्चास्मि नागानां वरुणो यादसामहम् ।

पितॄणामर्यमा चास्मि यमः संयमतामहम्

॥ १०-२९॥

Of the celestial Naga snakes I am Ananta; of the aquatic deities I am Varuna. Of departed ancestors I am Aryama, and among the dispensers of law I am Yama, lord of death.

प्रह्लादश्चास्मि दैत्यानां कालः कलयतामहम् ।
मृगाणां च मृगेन्द्रोऽहं वैनतेयश्च पक्षिणाम्

॥ १०-३० ॥

Among the Daitya demons I am the devoted Prahlada; among subduers I am time; among the beasts I am the lion, and among birds I am Garuda, the feathered carrier of Visnu.

पवनः पवतामस्मि रामः शस्त्रभृतामहम् ।
झषाणां मकरश्चास्मि स्रोतसामस्मि जाह्नवी

॥ १०-३१ ॥

Of purifiers I am the wind; of the wielders of weapons I am Rama; of fishes I am the shark, and of flowing rivers I am the Ganges.

सर्गाणामादिरन्तश्च मध्यं चैवाहमर्जुन ।
अध्यात्मविद्या विद्यानां वादः प्रवदतामहम्

॥ १०-३२ ॥

Of all creations I am the beginning and the end and also the middle, O Arjuna. Of all sciences I am the spiritual science of the Self, and among logicians I am the conclusive truth.

अक्षराणामकारोऽस्मि द्वन्द्वः सामासिकस्य च ।

अहमेवाक्षयः कालो धाताहं विश्वतोमुखः

॥ १०-३३॥

Of letters I am the letter A, and among compounds I am the dual word. I am also inexhaustable time, and of creators I am Brahma, whose manifold faces turn everywhere.

मृत्युः सर्वहरश्चाहमुद्भवश्च भविष्यताम् ।

कीर्तिः श्रीर्वाक्च नारीणां स्मृतिर्मेधा धृतिः क्षमा

॥ १०-३४॥

I am all-devouring death, and I am the generator of all things yet to be. Among women I am fame, fortune, speech, memory, intelligence, faithfulness and patience

बृहत्साम तथा साम्नां गायत्री छन्दसामहम् ।

मासानां मार्गशीर्षोऽहमृतूनां कुसुमाकरः

॥ १०-३५॥

Of hymns I am the Brhat-sama sung to the Lord Indra, and of poetry I am the Gayatri verse, sung daily by brahmanas. Of months I am November and December, and of seasons I am flower-bearing spring.

द्यूतं छलयतामस्मि तेजस्तेजस्विनामहम् ।

जयोऽस्मि व्यवसायोऽस्मि सत्त्वं सत्त्ववतामहम्

॥ १०-३६॥

I am also the gambling of cheats, and of the splendid I am the splendor. I am victory, I am adventure, and I am the strength of the strong.

वृष्णीनां वासुदेवोऽस्मि पाण्डवानां धनञ्जयः ।

मुनीनामप्यहं व्यासः कवीनामुशना कविः

॥ १०-३७॥

Of the descendants of Vrsni I am Vasudeva, and of the Pandavas I am Arjuna. Of the sages I am Vyasa, and among great thinkers I am Usana.

दण्डो दमयतामस्मि नीतिरस्मि जिगीषताम् ।

मौनं चैवास्मि गुह्यानां ज्ञानं ज्ञानवतामहम्

॥ १०-३८॥

Among punishments I am the rod of chastisement, and of those who seek victory, I am morality. Of secret things I am silence, and of the wise I am wisdom.

यच्चापि सर्वभूतानां बीजं तदहमर्जुन ।

न तदस्ति विना यत्स्यान्मया भूतं चराचरम्

॥ १०-३९॥

Furthermore, O Arjuna, I am the generating seed of all existences. There is no being-moving or unmoving-that can exist without Me.

नान्तोऽस्ति मम दिव्यानां विभूतीनां परन्तप ।

एष तूद्देशतः प्रोक्तो विभूतेर्विस्तरो मया

॥ १०-४०॥

O mighty conqueror of enemies, there is no end to My divine manifestations. What I have spoken to you is but a mere indication of My infinite opulences.

यद्यद्विभूतिमत्सत्त्वं श्रीमदूर्जितमेव वा ।

तत्तदेवावगच्छ त्वं मम तेजोंऽशसम्भवम्

॥ १०-४१॥

Know that all beautiful, glorious, and mighty creations spring from but a spark of My splendor.

अथवा बहुनैतेन किं ज्ञातेन तवार्जुन ।
विष्टभ्याहमिदं कृत्स्नमेकांशेन स्थितो जगत्

॥ १०-४२॥

What need is there for all this detailed knowledge, O Arjun? Simply know that by one fraction of my being, I pervade and support this entire creation.

ॐ तत्सदिति श्रीमद्भगवद्गीतासूपनिषत्सु
ब्रह्मविद्यायां योगशास्त्रे श्रीकृष्णार्जुनसंवादे
विभूतियोगो नाम दशमोऽध्यायः ॥ १०॥

अथैकादशोऽध्यायः । विश्वरूपदर्शनयोगः

HERE ENDETH CHAPTER X OF THE BHAGAVAD-GITA.

CHAPTER XI

In this chapter, Arjun requests to see Shree Krishna's viśhwarūp, or the infinite cosmic form of God that encompasses all the universes. Shree Krishna obliges by granting him divine vision. Arjun then sees the totality of creation in the body of the God of gods. He observes unlimited faces, eyes, arms, and stomachs in the wonderful and infinite form of the Lord.

The form has no beginning or end, and extends infinitely in every direction. The splendor of that form is more than a thousand suns blazing forth together in the sky. The vision makes Arjun's hair stand on end. He sees the three worlds trembling in fear of God's laws. He witnesses the celestial gods taking shelter of him and the great sages extolling him with profuse hymns and prayers.

He observers all the sons of Dhritarasthra along with their allied kings rushing headlong into the mouth of that fearsome form, as moths rushing with great speed into the fire to perish. Arjun then confesses that on beholding the universal form his heart is trembling with fear and he has lost his peace of mind.

अर्जुन उवाच ।

मदनुग्रहाय परमं गुह्यमध्यात्मसंज्ञितम् ।

यत्त्वयोक्तं वचस्तेन मोहोऽयं विगतो मम

॥ ११-१॥

Arjun said: Having heard the supremely confidential spiritual knowledge, which you have revealed out of compassion to me, my illusion is now dispelled.

भवाप्ययौ हि भूतानां श्रुतौ विस्तरशो मया ।

त्वत्तः कमलपत्राक्ष माहात्म्यमपि चाव्ययम्

॥ ११-२॥

I have heard from you in detail about the appearance and disappearance of all living beings, O lotus-eyed one, and also about your eternal majesty.

एवमेतद्यथात्थ त्वमात्मानं परमेश्वर ।

द्रष्टुमिच्छामि ते रूपमैश्वरं पुरुषोत्तम

॥ ११-३॥

O Supreme Lord, you are precisely what you declare yourself to be. Now I desire to see your divine cosmic form, O greatest of persons.

मन्यसे यदि तच्छक्यं मया द्रष्टुमिति प्रभो ।

योगेश्वर ततो मे त्वं दर्शयात्मानमव्ययम्

॥ ११-४॥

O Lord of all mystic powers, if you think I am strong enough to behold it, then kindly reveal that imperishable cosmic form to me.

श्रीभगवानुवाच ।

पश्य मे पार्थ रूपाणि शतशोऽथ सहस्रशः ।

नानाविधानि दिव्यानि नानावर्णाकृतीनि च

॥ ११-५॥

The Supreme Lord said: Behold, O Parth, my hundreds and thousands of wonderful forms of various shapes, sizes, and colors.

पश्यादित्यान्वसून्रुद्रानश्विनौ मरुतस्तथा ।

बहून्यदृष्टपूर्वाणि पश्याश्चर्याणि भारत

॥ ११-६॥

Behold in me, O scion of the Bharatas, the (twelve) sons of Aditi, the (eight) Vasus, the (eleven) Rudras, the (twin) Ashwini Kumars, as well as the (forty-nine) Maruts and many more marvels never revealed before.

इहैकस्थं जगत्कृत्स्नं पश्याद्य सचराचरम् ।

मम देहे गुडाकेश यच्चान्यद् द्रष्टुमिच्छसि

॥ ११-७॥

Behold now, Arjun, the entire universe, with everything moving and non-moving, assembled together in my universal form. Whatever else you wish to see, observe it all within this universal form.

न तु मां शक्यसे द्रष्टुमनेनैव स्वचक्षुषा ।

दिव्यं ददामि ते चक्षुः पश्य मे योगमैश्वरम्

॥ ११-८॥

But you cannot see my cosmic form with these physical eyes of yours. Therefore, I grant you divine vision. Behold my majestic opulence!

सञ्जय उवाच ।

एवमुक्त्वा ततो राजन्महायोगेश्वरो हरिः ।

दर्शयामास पार्थाय परमं रूपमैश्वरम्

॥ ११-९॥

Sanjay said: O King, having spoken thus, the Supreme Lord of Yog, Shree Krishna, displayed his divine and opulent form to Arjun.

अनेकवक्त्रनयनमनेकाद्भुतदर्शनम् ।

अनेकदिव्याभरणं दिव्यानेकोद्यतायुधम्

॥ ११-१०॥

दिव्यमाल्याम्बरधरं दिव्यगन्धानुलेपनम् ।

सर्वाश्चर्यमयं देवमनन्तं विश्वतोमुखम्

॥ ११-११॥

In that cosmic form, Arjun saw unlimited faces and eyes, decorated with many celestial ornaments and wielding many kinds of divine weapons. He wore many garlands on his body and was anointed with many sweet-smelling heavenly fragrances. He revealed himself as the wonderful and infinite Lord whose face is everywhere.

दिवि सूर्यसहस्रस्य भवेद्युगपदुत्थिता ।

यदि भाः सदृशी सा स्याद्भासस्तस्य महात्मनः

॥ ११-१२॥

If a thousand suns were to blaze forth together in the sky, they would not match the splendor of that great form.

तत्रैकस्थं जगत्कृत्स्नं प्रविभक्तमनेकधा ।

अपश्यद्देवदेवस्य शरीरे पाण्डवस्तदा

॥ ११-१३॥

There Arjun could see the totality of the entire universe established in one place, in that body of the God of gods.

ततः स विस्मयाविष्टो ह्रष्टरोमा धनञ्जयः ।

प्रणम्य शिरसा देवं कृताञ्जलिरभाषत

॥ ११-१४॥

Then, Arjun, full of wonder and with hair standing on end, bowed his head with folded hands before the Lord and addressed him thus.

अर्जुन उवाच ।

पश्यामि देवांस्तव देव देहे

सर्वांस्तथा भूतविशेषसङ्घान् ।

ब्रह्माणमीशं कमलासनस्थ-

मृषींश्च सर्वानुरगांश्च दिव्यान्

॥ ११-१५॥

Arjun said: O Shree Krishna, I behold within your body all the gods and hosts of different beings. I see Brahma seated on the lotus flower; I see Shiv, all the sages, and the celestial serpents.

अनेकबाहूदरवक्त्रनेत्रं

पश्यामि त्वां सर्वतोऽनन्तरूपम् ।

नान्तं न मध्यं न पुनस्तवादिं

पश्यामि विश्वेश्वर विश्वरूप

॥ ११-१६॥

I see your infinite form in every direction, with countless arms, stomachs, faces, and eyes. O Lord of the universe, whose form is the universe itself, I do not see in you any beginning, middle, or end.

किरीटिनं गदिनं चक्रिणं च

तेजोराशिं सर्वतो दीप्तिमन्तम् ।

पश्यामि त्वां दुर्निरीक्ष्यं समन्ताद्

दीप्तानलार्कद्युतिमप्रमेयम्

॥ ११-१७॥

I see your form, adorned with a crown, and armed with the club and disc, shining everywhere as the abode of splendor. It is hard to look upon you in the blazing fire of your effulgence, which is radiating like the sun in all directions.

त्वमक्षरं परमं वेदितव्यं

त्वमस्य विश्वस्य परं निधानम् ।

त्वमव्ययः शाश्वतधर्मगोप्ता

सनातनस्त्वं पुरुषो मतो मे

॥ ११-१८॥

I recognize you as the supreme imperishable being, the ultimate truth to be known by the scriptures. You are the support of all creation; you are the eternal protector of sanātan dharma (the eternal religion); and you are the everlasting Supreme Divine Personality.

अनादिमध्यान्तमनन्तवीर्य-

मनन्तबाहुं शशिसूर्यनेत्रम् ।

पश्यामि त्वां दीप्तहुताशवक्त्रं

स्वतेजसा विश्वमिदं तपन्तम्

॥ ११-१९॥

You are without beginning, middle, or end; your power has no limits. Your arms are infinite; the sun and the moon are like your eyes, and fire is like your mouth. I see you warming the entire creation by your radiance.

द्यावापृथिव्योरिदमन्तरं हि

व्याप्तं त्वयैकेन दिशश्च सर्वाः ।

दृष्ट्वाद्भुतं रूपमुग्रं तवेदं

लोकत्रयं प्रव्यथितं महात्मन्

॥ ११-२०॥

The space between heaven and earth and all the directions are pervaded by you alone. Seeing your wondrous and terrible form, I see the three worlds trembling in fear, O Greatest of all beings.

अमी हि त्वां सुरसङ्घा विशन्ति

केचिद्भीताः प्राञ्जलयो गृणन्ति ।

स्वस्तीत्युक्त्वा महर्षिसिद्धसङ्घाः

स्तुवन्ति त्वां स्तुतिभिः पुष्कलाभिः

॥ ११-२१॥

All the celestial gods are taking your shelter by entering into you. In awe, some are praising you with folded hands. The great sages and perfected beings are extolling you with auspicious hymns and profuse prayers.

रुद्रादित्या वसवो ये च साध्या

विश्वेऽश्विनौ मरुतश्चोष्मपाश्च ।

गन्धर्वयक्षासुरसिद्धसङ्घा

वीक्षन्ते त्वां विस्मिताश्चैव सर्वे

॥ ११-२२॥

The Rudras, Adityas, Vasus, Sadhyas, Vishvadevas, Ashwini Kumars, Maruts, ancestors, Gandharvas, Yakshas, Asuras, and Siddhas are all beholding you in wonder.

रूपं महत्ते बहुवक्त्रनेत्रं

महाबाहो बहुबाहूरुपादम् ।

बहूदरं बहुदंष्ट्राकरालं

दृष्ट्वा लोकाः प्रव्यथितास्तथाहम्

॥ ११-२३॥

O mighty Lord, in veneration of your magnificent form with its many mouths, eyes, arms, thighs, legs, stomachs, and terrifying teeth, all the worlds are terror-stricken, and so am I.

नभःस्पृशं दीप्तमनेकवर्णं

व्यात्ताननं दीप्तविशालनेत्रम् ।

दृष्ट्वा हि त्वां प्रव्यथितान्तरात्मा

धृतिं न विन्दामि शमं च विष्णो

॥ ११-२४॥

O Lord Vishnu, seeing your form touching the sky, effulgent in many colors, with mouths wide open and enormous blazing eyes, my heart is trembling with fear. I have lost all courage and peace of mind.

दंष्ट्राकरालानि च ते मुखानि

दृष्ट्वैव कालानलसन्निभानि ।

दिशो न जाने न लभे च शर्म

प्रसीद देवेश जगन्निवास

॥ ११-२५॥

Having seen your many mouths bearing your terrible teeth, resembling the raging fire at the time of annihilation, I forget where I am and do not know where to go. O Lord of lords, you are the shelter of the universe; please have mercy on me.

अमी च त्वां धृतराष्ट्रस्य पुत्राः

सर्वे सहैवावनिपालसङ्घैः ।

भीष्मो द्रोणः सूतपुत्रस्तथासौ

सहास्मदीयैरपि योधमुख्यैः

॥ ११-२६

वक्त्राणि ते त्वरमाणा विशन्ति

दंष्ट्राकरालानि भयानकानि ।

केचिद्विलग्ना दशनान्तरेषु

सन्दृश्यन्ते चूर्णितैरुत्तमाङ्गैः

॥ ११-२७॥

All the sons of Dhrtarastra along with their allied kings, and Bhisma, Drona and Karna, and all our soldiers are rushing into Your mouths, their heads smashed by Your fearful teeth. I see that some are being crushed between Your teeth as well.

यथा नदीनां बहवोऽम्बुवेगाः

समुद्रमेवाभिमुखा द्रवन्ति ।

तथा तवामी नरलोकवीरा

विशन्ति वक्त्राण्यभिविज्वलन्ति

॥ ११-२८॥

As the rivers flow into the sea, so all these great warriors enter Your blazing mouths and perish.

यथा प्रदीप्तं ज्वलनं पतङ्गा

विशन्ति नाशाय समृद्धवेगाः ।

तथैव नाशाय विशन्ति लोकास्-

तवापि वक्त्राणि समृद्धवेगाः

॥ ११-२९॥

I see all people rushing with full speed into Your mouths as moths dash into a blazing fire.

लेलिह्यसे ग्रसमानः समन्ताल्-

लोकान्समग्रान्वदनैर्ज्वलद्भिः ।

तेजोभिरापूर्य जगत्समग्रं

भासस्तवोग्राः प्रतपन्ति विष्णो

॥ ११-३० ॥

O Visnu, I see You devouring all people in Your flaming mouths and covering the universe with Your immeasurable rays. Scorching the worlds, You are manifest.

आख्याहि मे को भवानुग्ररूपो

नमोऽस्तु ते देववर प्रसीद ।

विज्ञातुमिच्छामि भवन्तमाद्यं

न हि प्रजानामि तव प्रवृत्तिम्

॥ ११-३१ ॥

O Lord of lords, so fierce of form, please tell me who You are. I offer my obeisances unto You; please be gracious to me. I do not know what Your mission is, and I desire to hear of it.

श्रीभगवानुवाच ।

कालोऽस्मि लोकक्षयकृत्प्रवृद्धो

लोकान्समाहर्तुमिह प्रवृत्तः ।

ऋतेऽपि त्वां न भविष्यन्ति सर्वे

येऽवस्थिताः प्रत्यनीकेषु योधाः

॥ ११-३२॥

The Blessed Lord said: Time I am, destroyer of the worlds, and I have come to engage all people. With the exception of you [the Pandavas], all the soldiers here on both sides will be slain.

तस्मात्त्वमुत्तिष्ठ यशो लभस्व

जित्वा शत्रून् भुङ्क्ष्व राज्यं समृद्धम् ।

मयैवैते निहताः पूर्वमेव

निमित्तमात्रं भव सव्यसाचिन्

॥ ११-३३॥

Therefore get up and prepare to fight. After conquering your enemies you will enjoy a flourishing kingdom. They are already put to death by My arrangement, and you, O Savyasacin, can be but an instmment in the fight.

द्रोणं च भीष्मं च जयद्रथं च

कर्णं तथान्यानपि योधवीरान् ।

मया हतांस्त्वं जहि मा व्यथिष्ठा

युध्यस्व जेतासि रणे सपत्नान्

॥ ११-३४॥

The Blessed Lord said: All the great warriors-Drona, Bhisma, Jayadratha, Karna-are already destroyed. Simply fight, and you will vanquish your enemies.

सञ्जय उवाच ।

एतच्छ्रुत्वा वचनं केशवस्य

कृताञ्जलिर्वेपमानः किरीटी ।

नमस्कृत्वा भूय एवाह कृष्णं

सगद्गदं भीतभीतः प्रणम्य

॥ ११-३५॥

Sanjaya said to Dhrtarastra: O King, after hearing these words from the Supreme Personality of Godhead, Arjuna trembled, fearfully offered obeisances with folded hands and began, falteringly, to speak as follows:

अर्जुन उवाच ।

स्थाने हृषीकेश तव प्रकीर्त्या

जगत्प्रहृष्यत्यनुरज्यते च ।

रक्षांसि भीतानि दिशो द्रवन्ति

सर्वे नमस्यन्ति च सिद्धसङ्घाः

॥ ११-३६ ॥

Arjun said: O Master of the senses, it is but apt that the universe rejoices in giving you praise and is enamored by You. Demons flee fearfully from you in all directions and the hosts of perfected saints bow to you.

कस्माच्च ते न नमेरन्महात्मन्

गरीयसे ब्रह्मणोऽप्यादिकर्त्रे ।

अनन्त देवेश जगन्निवास

त्वमक्षरं सदसत्तत्परं यत्

॥ ११-३७ ॥

O Great one, who are even greater than Brahma, the original creator, why should they not bow to you? O limitless One, O Lord of the devatās, O Refuge of the universe, you are the imperishable reality beyond both the manifest and the non-manifest.

त्वमादिदेवः पुरुषः पुराणस्-

त्वमस्य विश्वस्य परं निधानम् ।

वेत्तासि वेद्यं च परं च धाम

त्वया ततं विश्वमनन्तरूप

॥ ११-३८॥

You are the primeval God and the original Divine Personality; you are the sole resting place of this universe. You are both the knower and the object of knowledge; you are the Supreme Abode. O possessor of infinite forms, you alone pervade the entire universe.

वायुर्यमोऽग्निर्वरुणः शशाङ्कः

प्रजापतिस्त्वं प्रपितामहश्च ।

नमो नमस्तेऽस्तु सहस्रकृत्वः

पुनश्च भूयोऽपि नमो नमस्ते

॥ ११-३९॥

You are Vāyu (the god of wind), Yamraj (the god of death), Agni (the god of fire), Varuṇ (the god of water), and Chandra (the moon-God). You are the creator Brahma, and the great-grandfather of all beings. I offer my salutations unto you a thousand times, again and yet again!

नम: पुरस्तादथ पृष्ठतस्ते

नमोऽस्तु ते सर्वत एव सर्व ।

अनन्तवीर्यामितविक्रमस्त्वं

सर्वं समाप्नोषि ततोऽसि सर्व:

॥ ११-४० ॥

O Lord of infinite power, my salutations to you from the front and the rear, indeed from all sides! You possess infinite valor and might and pervade everything, and thus, you are everything.

सखेति मत्वा प्रसभं यदुक्तं

हे कृष्ण हे यादव हे सखेति ।

अजानता महिमानं तवेदं

मया प्रमादात्प्रणयेन वापि

॥ ११-४१ ॥

यच्चावहासार्थमसत्कृतोऽसि
विहारशय्यासनभोजनेषु ।
एकोऽथवाप्यच्युत तत्समक्षं
तत्क्षामये त्वामहमप्रमेयम्
॥ ११-४२ ॥

Thinking of you as my friend, I presumptuously addressed you as, "O Krishna," "O Yadav," "O my dear mate." I was ignorant of your majesty, showing negligence and undue affection. And if, jestfully, I t reated you with disrespect, while playing, resting, sitting, eating, when alone, or before others—for all that I crave forgiveness.

पितासि लोकस्य चराचरस्य
त्वमस्य पूज्यश्च गुरुर्गरीयान् ।
न त्वत्समोऽस्त्यभ्यधिक: कुतोऽन्यो
लोकत्रयेऽप्यप्रतिमप्रभाव
॥ ११-४३ ॥

You are the father of the entire universe, of all moving and non-moving beings. You are the most deserving of worship and the supreme spiritual master. When there is none equal to you in all the three worlds, then who can possibly be greater than you, O possessor of incomparable power?

तस्मात्प्रणम्य प्रणिधाय कायं

प्रसादये त्वामहमीशमीड्यम् ।

पितेव पुत्रस्य सखेव सख्यु:

प्रिय: प्रियायार्हसि देव सोढुम्

॥ ११-४४ ॥

Therefore, O adorable Lord, bowing deeply and prostrating before you, I implore you for your grace. As a father tolerates his son, a friend forgives his friend, and a lover pardons the beloved, please forgive me for my offences.

अदृष्टपूर्वं हृषितोऽस्मि दृष्ट्वा

भयेन च प्रव्यथितं मनो मे ।

तदेव मे दर्शय देवरूपं

प्रसीद देवेश जगन्निवास

॥ ११-४५ ॥

Having seen your universal form that I had never seen before, I feel great joy. And yet, my mind trembles with fear. Please have mercy on me and again show me your pleasing form, O God of gods, O abode of the universe.

किरीटिनं गदिनं चक्रहस्त-

मिच्छामि त्वां द्रष्टुमहं तथैव ।

तेनैव रूपेण चतुर्भुजेन

सहस्रबाहो भव विश्वमूर्ते

॥ ११-४६ ॥

O thousand-armed one, though you are the embodiment of all creation, I wish to see you in your four-armed form, carrying the mace and disc, and wearing the crown.

श्रीभगवानुवाच ।

मया प्रसन्नेन तवार्जुनेदं

रूपं परं दर्शितमात्मयोगात् ।

तेजोमयं विश्वमनन्तमाद्यं

यन्मे त्वदन्येन न दृष्टपूर्वम्

॥ ११-४७॥

The Blessed Lord said: Arjun, being pleased with you, by my Yogmaya power, I gave you a vision of my resplendent, unlimited, and primeval cosmic form. No one before you has ever seen it.

न वेदयज्ञाध्ययनैर्न दानैर्-

न च क्रियाभिर्न तपोभिरुग्रैः ।

एवंरूपः शक्य अहं नृलोके

द्रष्टुं त्वदन्येन कुरुप्रवीर

॥ ११-४८॥

Not by study of the Vedas, nor by the performance of sacrifice, rituals, or charity, nor even by practicing severe austerities, has any mortal ever seen what you have seen, O best of the Kuru warriors.

मा ते व्यथा मा च विमूढभावो

दृष्ट्वा रूपं घोरमीदृङ्ममेदम् ।

व्यपेतभीः प्रीतमनाः पुनस्त्वं

तदेव मे रूपमिदं प्रपश्य

॥ ११-४९॥

Be neither afraid nor bewildered on seeing this terrible form of mine. Be free from fear and with a cheerful heart, behold me once again in my personal form.

सञ्जय उवाच ।

इत्यर्जुनं वासुदेवस्तथोक्त्वा

स्वकं रूपं दर्शयामास भूयः ।

आश्वासयामास च भीतमेनं

भूत्वा पुनः सौम्यवपुर्महात्मा

॥ ११-५०॥

Sanjay said: Having spoken thus, the compassionate son of Vasudev displayed his personal (four-armed) form again. Then, he further consoled the frightened Arjun by assuming his gentle (two-armed) form.

अर्जुन उवाच ।

दृष्ट्वेदं मानुषं रूपं तव सौम्यं जनार्दन ।

इदानीमस्मि संवृत्तः सचेताः प्रकृतिं गतः

॥ ११-५१॥

Arjun said: O Shree Krishna, seeing your gentle human form (two-armed), I have regained my composure and my mind is restored to normal.

श्रीभगवानुवाच ।

सुदुर्दर्शमिदं रूपं दृष्टवानसि यन्मम ।

देवा अप्यस्य रूपस्य नित्यं दर्शनकाङ्क्षिणः

॥ ११-५२॥

The Blessed Lord said: My dear Arjuna, the form which you are now seeing is very difficult to behold. Even the demigods are ever seeking the opportunity to see this form which is so dear.

नाहं वेदैर्न तपसा न दानेन न चेज्यया ।

शक्य एवंविधो द्रष्टुं दृष्टवानसि मां यथा

॥ ११-५३॥

The form which you are seeing with your transcendental eyes cannot be understood simply by studying the Vedas, nor by undergoing serious penances, nor by charity, nor by worship. It is not by these means that one can see Me as I am.

भक्त्या त्वनन्यया शक्य अहमेवंविधोऽर्जुन ।

ज्ञातुं द्रष्टुं च तत्त्वेन प्रवेष्टुं च परन्तप

॥ ११-५४॥

O Arjun, by unalloyed devotion alone can I be known as I am, standing before you. Thereby, on receiving my divine vision, O scorcher of foes, one can enter into union with me.

मत्कर्मकृन्मत्परमो मद्भक्तः सङ्गवर्जितः ।

निर्वैरः सर्वभूतेषु यः स मामेति पाण्डव

॥ ११-५५॥

Those who perform all their duties for my sake, who depend upon me and are devoted to me, who are free from attachment, and are without malice toward all beings, such devotees certainly come to me.

ॐ तत्सदिति श्रीमद्भगवद्गीतासूपनिषत्सु

ब्रह्मविद्यायां योगशास्त्रे श्रीकृष्णार्जुनसंवादे

विश्वरूपदर्शनयोगो नामैकादशोऽध्यायः

॥ ११॥

अथ द्वादशोऽध्यायः ।   भक्तियोगः

HERE ENDETH CHAPTER XI OF THE BHAGAVAD-GITA.

CHAPTER XII

This small chapter stresses on the super-excellence of the path of loving devotion over all other types of spiritual practices. It begins with Arjun asking Shree Krishna whom He considers more perfect in Yog—those who are devoted to the personal form of God or those who worship the formless Brahman. Shree Krishna responds by declaring that both paths lead to God-realization. However, He regards the devotees of His personal form as the best yogis.

He explains that meditation on the impersonal unmanifest aspect of God is full of tribulations and is exceedingly difficult for embodied beings. But devotees of the personal form, with their consciousness merged in Him and all their actions dedicated to Him, are swifly delivered from the cycle of life and death.

Shree Krishna thus asks Arjun to surrender his intellect to Him, and fix his mind in exclusive loving devotion on Him alone.

अर्जुन उवाच ।

एवं सततयुक्ता ये भक्तास्त्वां पर्युपासते ।
ये चाप्यक्षरमव्यक्तं तेषां के योगवित्तमाः
॥ १२-१॥

Arjun inquired: Between those who are steadfastly devoted to Your personal form and those who worship the formless Brahman, who do You consider to be more perfect in Yog?

श्रीभगवानुवाच ।

मय्यावेश्य मनो ये मां नित्ययुक्ता उपासते ।
श्रद्धया परयोपेताः ते मे युक्ततमा मताः
॥ १२-२॥

The Blessed Lord said: Those who fix their minds on Me and always engage in My devotion with steadfast faith, I consider them to be the best yogis.

ये त्वक्षरमनिर्देश्यमव्यक्तं पर्युपासते ।

सर्वत्रगमचिन्त्यञ्च कूटस्थमचलन्ध्रुवम्

॥ १२-३॥

सन्नियम्येन्द्रियग्रामं सर्वत्र समबुद्धयः ।

ते प्राप्नुवन्ति मामेव सर्वभूतहिते रताः

॥ १२-४॥

But those who worship the formless aspect of the Absolute Truth—the imperishable, the indefinable, the unmanifest, the all-pervading, the unthinkable, the unchanging, the eternal, and the immoveable—by restraining their senses and being even-minded everywhere, such persons, engaged in the welfare of all beings, also attain Me.

क्लेशोऽधिकतरस्तेषामव्यक्तासक्तचेतसाम् ।

अव्यक्ता हि गतिर्दुःखं देहवद्भिरवाप्यते

॥ १२-५॥

For those whose minds are attached to the unmanifest, the path of realization is full of tribulations. Worship of the unmanifest is exceedingly difficult for embodied beings.

ये तु सर्वाणि कर्माणि मयि संन्यस्य मत्पराः ।

अनन्येनैव योगेन मां ध्यायन्त उपासते ॥ १२-६॥

तेषामहं समुद्धर्ता मृत्युसंसारसागरात् ।

भवामि नचिरात्पार्थ मय्यावेशितचेतसाम्

॥ १२-७॥

But those who dedicate all their actions to Me, regarding Me as the Supreme goal, worshiping Me and meditating on Me with exclusive devotion, O Parth, I swiftly deliver them from the ocean of birth and death, for their consciousness is united with Me.

मय्येव मन आधत्स्व मयि बुद्धिं निवेशय ।

निवसिष्यसि मय्येव अत ऊर्ध्वं न संशयः

॥ १२-८॥

Fix your mind on Me alone and surrender your intellect to Me. There upon, you will always live in Me. Of this, there is no doubt.

अथ चित्तं समाधातुं न शक्नोषि मयि स्थिरम् ।

अभ्यासयोगेन ततो मामिच्छाप्तुं धनञ्जय

॥ १२-९॥

If you are unable to fix your mind steadily on Me, O Arjun, then practice remembering Me with devotion while constantly restraining the mind from worldly affairs.

अभ्यासेऽप्यसमर्थोऽसि मत्कर्मपरमो भव ।

मदर्थमपि कर्माणि कुर्वन्सिद्धिमवाप्स्यसि

॥ १२-१०॥

If you cannot practice remembering Me with devotion, then just try to work for Me. Thus performing devotional service to Me, you shall achieve the stage of perfection.

अथैतदप्यशक्तोऽसि कर्तुं मद्योगमाश्रितः ।

सर्वकर्मफलत्यागं ततः कुरु यतात्मवान्

॥ १२-११॥

If you are unable to even work for Me in devotion, then try to renounce the fruits of your actions and be situated in the self.

श्रेयो हि ज्ञानमभ्यासाज्ज्ञानाद्ध्यानं विशिष्यते ।
ध्यानात्कर्मफलत्यागस्त्यागाच्छान्तिरनन्तरम्

॥ १२-१२॥

Better than mechanical practice is knowledge; better than knowledge is meditation. Better than meditation is renunciation of the fruits of actions, for peace immediately follows such renunciation.

अद्वेष्टा सर्वभूतानां मैत्रः करुण एव च ।
निर्ममो निरहङ्कारः समदुःखसुखः क्षमी

॥ १२-१३॥

सन्तुष्टः सततं योगी यतात्मा दृढनिश्चयः ।
मय्यर्पितमनोबुद्धिर्यो मद्भक्तः स मे प्रियः

॥ १२-१४॥

Those devotees are very dear to Me who are free from malice toward all living beings, who are friendly, and compassionate. They are free from attachment to possessions and egotism, equipoised in happiness and distress, and ever-forgiving. They are ever-contented, steadily united with Me in devotion, self-controlled, firm in conviction, and dedicated to Me in mind and intellect.

यस्मान्नोद्विजते लोको लोकान्नोद्विजते च यः ।
हर्षामर्षभयोद्वेगैर्मुक्तो यः स च मे प्रियः
॥ १२-१५॥

Those who are not a source of annoyance to anyone and who in turn are not agitated by anyone, who are equal in pleasure and pain, and free from fear and anxiety, such devotees of Mine are very dear to Me.

अनपेक्षः शुचिर्दक्ष उदासीनो गतव्यथः ।
सर्वारम्भपरित्यागी यो मद्भक्तः स मे प्रियः
॥ १२-१६॥

Those who are indifferent to worldly gain, externally and internally pure, skillful, without cares, untroubled, and free from selfishness in all undertakings, such devotees of Mine are very dear to Me.

यो न हृष्यति न द्वेष्टि न शोचति न काङ्क्षति ।

शुभाशुभपरित्यागी भक्तिमान्यः स मे प्रियः

॥ १२-१७॥

Those who neither rejoice in mundane pleasures nor despair in worldly sorrows, who neither lament for any loss nor hanker for any gain, who renounce both good and evil deeds, such persons who are full of devotion are very dear to Me.

समः शत्रौ च मित्रे च तथा मानापमानयोः ।

शीतोष्णसुखदुःखेषु समः सङ्गविवर्जितः

॥ १२-१८॥

तुल्यनिन्दास्तुतिर्मौनी सन्तुष्टो येन केनचित् ।

अनिकेतः स्थिरमतिर्भक्तिमान्मे प्रियो नरः

॥ १२-१९॥

Those, who are alike to friend and foe, equipoised in honor and dishonor, cold and heat, joy and sorrow, and are free from all unfavorable association; those who take praise and reproach alike, who are given to silent contemplation, content with what comes their way, without attachment to the place of residence, whose intellect is firmly fixed in Me, and who are full of devotion to Me, such persons are very dear to Me.

ये तु धर्म्यामृतमिदं यथोक्तं पर्युपासते ।

श्रद्दधाना मत्परमा भक्तास्तेऽतीव मे प्रियाः

॥ १२-२०॥

Those who honor this nectar of wisdom declared here, have faith in Me, and are devoted and intent on Me as the supreme goal, they are exceedingly dear to Me.

ॐ तत्सदिति श्रीमद्भगवद्गीतासूपनिषत्सु

ब्रह्मविद्यायां योगशास्त्रे श्रीकृष्णार्जुनसंवादे

भक्तियोगो नाम द्वादशोऽध्यायः

॥ १२॥

अथ त्रयोदशोऽध्यायः । क्षेत्रक्षेत्रज्ञविभागयोगः

HERE ENDETH CHAPTER XII OF THE BHAGAVAD-GITA.

CHAPTER XIII

In the present chapter, Shree Krishna goes into a detailed analysis of this distinction. He enumerates the elements of material nature that compose the field of the body. He describes the modifications that arise in the field, in the form of emotions, sentiments, and feelings. He also mentions the virtues and qualities that purify the field and illumine it with the light of knowledge. Such knowledge helps us gain realization of the soul, who is the knower of the field. The chapter then describes God, who is the supreme knower of the fields of all the living beings.

That Supreme Lord holds contradictory attributes, i.e. He possesses opposite qualities at the same time. So, He is all-pervading in creation and yet seated in the hearts of all living beings. He is thus the Supreme Soul of all living beings.

Having described the soul, the Supreme Soul, and matrial nature, Shree Krishna then explains which of these is responsible for actions by living beings, and also which is responsible for cause and effect in the world at large.

अर्जुन उवाच ।

प्रकृतिं पुरुषं चैव क्षेत्रं क्षेत्रज्ञमेव च ।

एतद्वेदितुमिच्छामि ज्ञानं ज्ञेयं च केशव ॥ १३-१॥

Arjun said, "O Keshav, I wish to understand what are prakṛiti and puruṣh, and what are kṣhetra and kṣhetrajña? I also wish to know what is true knowledge, and what is the goal of this knowledge?

श्रीभगवानुवाच ।

इदं शरीरं कौन्तेय क्षेत्रमित्यभिधीयते ।

एतद्यो वेत्ति तं प्राहुः क्षेत्रज्ञ इति तद्विदः ॥ १३-२॥

The Supreme Divine Lord said: O Arjun, this body is termed as kṣhetra (the field of activities), and the one who knows this body is called kṣhetrajña (the knower of the field) by the sages who discern the truth about both.

क्षेत्रज्ञं चापि मां विद्धि सर्वक्षेत्रेषु भारत ।

क्षेत्रक्षेत्रज्ञयोर्ज्ञानं यत्तज्ज्ञानं मतं मम ॥ १३-३॥

O scion of Bharat, I am also the knower of all the individual fields of activity. The understanding of the body as the field of activities, and the soul and God as the knowers of the field, this I hold to be true knowledge.

तत्क्षेत्रं यच्च यादृक्च यद्विकारि यतश्च यत् ।

स च यो यत्प्रभावश्च तत्समासेन मे शृणु ॥ १३-४॥

Listen and I will explain to you what that field is and what its nature is. I will also explain how change takes place within it, from what it was created, who the knower of the field of activities is, and what his powers are.

ऋषिभिर्बहुधा गीतं छन्दोभिर्विविधैः पृथक् ।

ब्रह्मसूत्रपदैश्चैव हेतुमद्भिर्विनिश्चितैः ॥ १३-५॥

Great sages have sung the truth about the field and the knower of the field in manifold ways. It has been stated in various Vedic hymns, and especially revealed in the Brahma Sūtra, with sound logic and conclusive evidence.

महाभूतान्यहङ्कारो बुद्धिरव्यक्तमेव च ।

इन्द्रियाणि दशैकं च पञ्च चेन्द्रियगोचराः

॥ १३-६ ॥

The field of activities is composed of the five great elements, the ego, the intellect, the unmanifest primordial matter, the eleven senses (five knowledge senses, five working senses, and mind), and the five objects of the senses.

इच्छा द्वेषः सुखं दुःखं सङ्घातश्चेतना धृतिः ।

एतत्क्षेत्रं समासेन सविकारमुदाहृतम्

॥ १३-७ ॥

Desire and aversion, happiness and misery, the body, consciousness, and the will—all these comprise the field and its modifications.

अमानित्वमदम्भित्वमहिंसा क्षान्तिरार्जवम् ।

आचार्योपासनं शौचं स्थैर्यमात्मविनिग्रहः ॥ १३-८॥

इन्द्रियार्थेषु वैराग्यमनहङ्कार एव च ।

जन्ममृत्युजराव्याधिदुःखदोषानुदर्शनम् ॥ १३-९॥

असक्तिरनभिष्वङ्गः पुत्रदारगृहादिषु ।

नित्यं च समचित्तत्वमिष्टानिष्टोपपत्तिषु ॥ १३-१०॥

मयि चानन्ययोगेन भक्तिरव्यभिचारिणी ।

विविक्तदेशसेवित्वमरतिर्जनसंसदि ॥ १३-११॥

अध्यात्मज्ञाननित्यत्वं तत्त्वज्ञानार्थदर्शनम् ।

एतज्ज्ञानमिति प्रोक्तमज्ञानं यदतोऽन्यथा ॥ १३-१२॥

Humbleness; freedom from hypocrisy; non-violence; forgiveness; simplicity; service of the Guru; cleanliness of body and mind; steadfastness; and self-control; dispassion toward the objects of the senses; absence of egotism; keeping in mind the evils of birth, disease, old age, and death; non-attachment; absence of clinging to spouse, children, home, and so on; even-mindedness amidst desired and undesired events in life; constant and exclusive devotion toward Me; an inclination for solitary places and an aversion for mundane society; constancy in spiritual knowledge; and philosophical pursuit of the Absolute Truth—all these I declare to be knowledge, and what is contrary to it, I call ignorance.

ज्ञेयं यत्तत्प्रवक्ष्यामि यज्ज्ञात्वामृतमश्नुते ।

अनादिमत्परं ब्रह्म न सत्तन्नासदुच्यते

॥ १३-१३॥

I shall now reveal to you that which ought to be known, and by knowing which, one attains immortality. It is the beginningless Brahman, which lies beyond existence and non-existence.

सर्वतः पाणिपादं तत्सर्वतोऽक्षिशिरोमुखम् ।

सर्वतः श्रुतिमल्लोके सर्वमावृत्य तिष्ठति

॥ १३-१४॥

Everywhere are His hands and feet, eyes, heads, and faces. His ears too are in all places, for He pervades everything in the universe.

सर्वेन्द्रियगुणाभासं सर्वेन्द्रियविवर्जितम् ।

असक्तं सर्वभृच्चैव निर्गुणं गुणभोक्तृ च

॥ १३-१५॥

Though He perceives all sense-objects, yet He is devoid of the senses. He is unattached to anything, and yet He is the sustainer of all. Although He is without attributes, yet He is the enjoyer of the three modes of material nature.

बहिरन्तश्च भूतानामचरं चरमेव च ।
सूक्ष्मत्वात्तदविज्ञेयं दूरस्थं चान्तिके च तत्

॥ १३-१६॥

He exists outside and inside all living beings, those that are moving and not moving. He is subtle, and hence, He is incomprehensible. He is very far, but He is also very near.

अविभक्तं च भूतेषु विभक्तमिव च स्थितम् ।
भूतभर्तृ च तज्ज्ञेयं ग्रसिष्णु प्रभविष्णु च

॥ १३-१७॥

He is indivisible, yet He appears to be divided amongst living beings. Know the Supreme Entity to be the Sustainer, Annihilator, and Creator of all beings.

ज्योतिषामपि तज्ज्योतिस्तमसः परमुच्यते ।
ज्ञानं ज्ञेयं ज्ञानगम्यं हृदि सर्वस्य विष्ठितम्

॥ १३-१८॥

He is the source of light in all luminaries, and is entirely beyond the darkness of ignorance. He is knowledge, the object of knowledge, and the goal of knowledge. He dwells within the hearts of all living beings.

इति क्षेत्रं तथा ज्ञानं ज्ञेयं चोक्तं समासतः ।

मद्भक्त एतद्विज्ञाय मद्भावायोपपद्यते

॥ १३-१९॥

I have thus revealed to you the nature of the field, the meaning of knowledge, and the object of knowledge. Only My devotees can understand this in reality, and by doing so, they attain My divine nature.

प्रकृतिं पुरुषं चैव विद्ध्यनादी उभावपि ।

विकारांश्च गुणांश्चैव विद्धि प्रकृतिसम्भवान्

॥ १३-२०॥

Know that prakṛiti (material nature) and puruṣh (the individual souls) are both beginningless. Also know that all transformations of the body and the three modes of nature are produced by material energy.

कार्यकारणकर्तृत्वे हेतुः प्रकृतिरुच्यते ।

पुरुषः सुखदुःखानां भोक्तृत्वे हेतुरुच्यते

॥ १३-२१॥

In the matter of creation, the material energy is responsible for cause and effect; in the matter of experiencing happiness and distress, the individual soul is declared responsible.

पुरुषः प्रकृतिस्थो हि भुङ्क्ते प्रकृतिजान्गुणान् ।

कारणं गुणसङ्गोऽस्य सदसद्योनिजन्मसु

॥ १३-२२॥

When the purușh (individual soul) seated in prakṛiti (the material energy) desires to enjoy the three guṇas, attachment to them becomes the cause of its birth in superior and inferior wombs.

उपद्रष्टानुमन्ता च भर्ता भोक्ता महेश्वरः ।

परमात्मेति चाप्युक्तो देहेऽस्मिन्पुरुषः परः

॥ १३-२३॥

Within the body also resides the Supreme Lord. He is said to be the Witness, the Permitter, the Supporter, Transcendental Enjoyer, the ultimate Controller, and the Paramātmā (Supreme Soul).

य एवं वेत्ति पुरुषं प्रकृतिं च गुणैः सह ।
सर्वथा वर्तमानोऽपि न स भूयोऽभिजायते

॥ १३-२४॥

Those who understand the truth about Supreme Soul, the individual soul, material nature, and the interaction of the three modes of nature will not take birth here again. They will be liberated regardless of their present condition.

ध्यानेनात्मनि पश्यन्ति केचिदात्मानमात्मना ।
अन्ये साङ्ख्येन योगेन कर्मयोगेन चापरे

॥ १३-२५॥

Some try to perceive the Supreme Soul within their hearts through meditation, and others try to do so through the cultivation of knowledge, while still others strive to attain that realization by the path of action.

अन्ये त्वेवमजानन्तः श्रुत्वान्येभ्य उपासते ।

तेऽपि चातितरन्त्येव मृत्युं श्रुतिपरायणाः

॥ १३-२६॥

There are still others who are unaware of these spiritual paths, but they hear from others and begin worshipping the Supreme Lord. By such devotion to hearing from saints, they too can gradually cross over the ocean of birth and death.

यावत्सञ्जायते किञ्चित्सत्त्वं स्थावरजङ्गमम् ।

क्षेत्रक्षेत्रज्ञसंयोगात्तद्विद्धि भरतर्षभ

॥ १३-२७॥

O best of the Bharatas, whatever moving or unmoving being you see in existence, know it to be a combination of the field of activities and the knower of the field.

समं सर्वेषु भूतेषु तिष्ठन्तं परमेश्वरम् ।

विनश्यत्स्वविनश्यन्तं यः पश्यति स पश्यति

॥ १३-२८॥

They alone truly see, who perceive the Paramātmā (Supreme Soul) accompanying the soul in all beings, and who understand both to be imperishable in this perishable body.

समं पश्यन्हि सर्वत्र समवस्थितमीश्वरम् ।

न हिनस्त्यात्मनात्मानं ततो याति परां गतिम्

॥ १३-२९॥

Those, who see God as the Supreme Soul equally present everywhere and in all living beings, do not degrade themselves by their mind. Thereby, they reach the supreme destination.

प्रकृत्यैव च कर्माणि क्रियमाणानि सर्वशः ।

यः पश्यति तथात्मानमकर्तारं स पश्यति

॥ १३-३०॥

They alone truly see who understand that all actions (of the body) are performed by material nature, while the embodied soul actually does nothing.

यदा भूतपृथग्भावमेकस्थमनुपश्यति ।

तत एव च विस्तारं ब्रह्म सम्पद्यते तदा

॥ १३-३१॥

When they see the diverse variety of living beings situated in the same material nature, and understand all of them to be born from it, they attain the realization of Brahman.

अनादित्वान्निर्गुणत्वात्परमात्मायमव्ययः ।

शरीरस्थोऽपि कौन्तेय न करोति न लिप्यते

॥ १३-३२॥

The Supreme Soul is imperishable, without beginning, and devoid of any material qualities, O son of Kunti. Although situated within the body, It neither acts, nor is It tainted by material energy.

यथा सर्वगतं सौक्ष्म्यादाकाशं नोपलिप्यते ।

सर्वत्रावस्थितो देहे तथात्मा नोपलिप्यते

॥ १३-३३॥

Space holds everything within it, but being subtle, does not get contaminated by what it holds. Similarly, though its consciousness pervades the body, the soul is not affected by the attributes of the body.

यथा प्रकाशयत्येकः कृत्स्नं लोकमिमं रविः ।

क्षेत्रं क्षेत्री तथा कृत्स्नं प्रकाशयति भारत

॥ १३-३४॥

Just as one sun illumines the entire solar system, so does the individual soul illumine the entire body (with consciousness).

क्षेत्रक्षेत्रज्ञयोरेवमन्तरं ज्ञानचक्षुषा ।
भूतप्रकृतिमोक्षं च ये विदुर्यान्ति ते परम्

॥ १३-३५॥

Those who perceive with the eyes of knowledge the difference between the body and the knower of the body, and the process of release from material nature, attain the supreme destination.

ॐ तत्सदिति श्रीमद्भगवद्गीतासूपनिषत्सु
ब्रह्मविद्यायां योगशास्त्रे श्रीकृष्णार्जुनसंवादे
क्षेत्रक्षेत्रज्ञविभागयोगो नाम त्रयोदशोऽध्यायः

॥ १३॥

HERE ENDS CHAPTER XIII OF THE BHAGAVAD-GITA.

CHAPTER XIV

This chapter describes the nature of the material energy, which is the source of the body and its elements, and is thus the origin of both mind and matter. Shree Krishna explains that material nature is constituted of three modes — goodness, passion, and ignorance. The body, mind, and intellect that are made from the material energy also possess these three modes, and the mix of the modes in our being determines the color of our personality. The mode of goodness is characterized by peacefulness, well-being, virtue, and serenity; the mode of passion gives rise to endless desires and insatiable ambitions for worldly enhancement; and the mode of ignorance is the cause for delusion, laziness, intoxication, and sleep. Until the soul attains illumination, it must learn to deal with these three powerful forces of material nature. Liberation lies in transcending all three of these modes.

Shree Krishna reveals a simple solution for breaking out of the bondages. The Supreme Lord is transcendental to the three modes, and if we attach ourselves to him, then our mind will also rise to the divine platform.

श्रीभगवानुवाच ।

परं भूयः प्रवक्ष्यामि ज्ञानानां ज्ञानमुत्तमम् ।

यज्ज्ञात्वा मुनयः सर्वे परां सिद्धिमितो गताः

॥ १४-१॥

The Divine Lord said: I shall once again explain to you the supreme wisdom, the best of all knowledge; by knowing which, all the great saints attained the highest perfection.

इदं ज्ञानमुपाश्रित्य मम साधर्म्यमागताः ।

सर्गेऽपि नोपजायन्ते प्रलये न व्यथन्ति च

॥ १४-२॥

Those who take refuge in this wisdom will be united with me. They will not be reborn at the time of creation nor destroyed at the time of dissolution.

मम योनिर्महद् ब्रह्म तस्मिन्गर्भं दधाम्यहम् ।
सम्भवः सर्वभूतानां ततो भवति भारत

॥ १४-३॥

सर्वयोनिषु कौन्तेय मूर्तयः सम्भवन्ति याः ।
तासां ब्रह्म महद्योनिरहं बीजप्रदः पिता

॥ १४-४॥

The total material substance, prakṛiti, is the womb. I impregnate it with the individual souls, and thus all living beings are born. O son of Kunti, for all species of life that are produced, the material nature is the womb, and I am the seed-giving Father.

सत्त्वं रजस्तम इति गुणाः प्रकृतिसम्भवाः ।
निबध्नन्ति महाबाहो देहे देहिनमव्ययम्

॥ १४-५॥

O mighty-armed Arjun, the material energy consists of three guṇas (modes)—sattva (goodness), rajas (passion), and tamas (ignorance). These modes bind the eternal soul to the perishable body.

तत्र सत्त्वं निर्मलत्वात्प्रकाशकमनामयम् ।

सुखसङ्गेन बध्नाति ज्ञानसङ्गेन चानघ

॥ १४-६॥

Amongst these, sattva guṇa, the mode of goodness, being purer than the others, is illuminating and full of well-being. O sinless one, it binds the soul by creating attachment for a sense of happiness and knowledge.

रजो रागात्मकं विद्धि तृष्णासङ्गसमुद्भवम् ।

तन्निबध्नाति कौन्तेय कर्मसङ्गेन देहिनम्

॥ १४-७॥

O Arjun, rajo guṇa is of the nature of passion. It arises from worldly desires and affections, and binds the soul through attachment to fruitive actions.

तमस्त्वज्ञानजं विद्धि मोहनं सर्वदेहिनाम् ।

प्रमादालस्यनिद्राभिस्तन्निबध्नाति भारत

॥ १४-८॥

O Arjun, tamo guṇa, which is born of ignorance, is the cause of illusion for the embodied souls. It deludes all living beings through negligence, laziness, and sleep.

सत्त्वं सुखे सञ्जयति रजः कर्मणि भारत ।

ज्ञानमावृत्य तु तमः प्रमादे सञ्जयत्युत

॥ १४-९॥

Sattva binds one to material happiness; rajas conditions the soul toward actions; and tamas clouds wisdom and binds one to delusion.

रजस्तमश्चाभिभूय सत्त्वं भवति भारत ।

रजः सत्त्वं तमश्चैव तमः सत्त्वं रजस्तथा

॥ १४-१०॥

Sometimes goodness (sattva) prevails over passion (rajas) and ignorance (tamas), O scion of Bharat. Sometimes passion (rajas) dominates goodness (sattva) and ignorance (tamas), and at other times ignorance (tamas) overcomes goodness (sattva) and passion (rajas).

सर्वद्वारेषु देहेऽस्मिन्प्रकाश उपजायते ।

ज्ञानं यदा तदा विद्याद्विवृद्धं सत्त्वमित्युत

॥ १४-११॥

लोभः प्रवृत्तिरारम्भः कर्मणामशमः स्पृहा ।

रजस्येतानि जायन्ते विवृद्धे भरतर्षभ

॥ १४-१२॥

अप्रकाशोऽप्रवृत्तिश्च प्रमादो मोह एव च ।

तमस्येतानि जायन्ते विवृद्धे कुरुनन्दन

॥ १४-१३॥

When all the gates of the body are illumined by knowledge, know it to be a manifestation of the mode of goodness. When the mode of passion predominates, O Arjun, the symptoms of greed, exertion for worldly gain, restlessness, and craving develop. O Arjun, nescience, inertia, negligence, and delusion—these are the dominant signs of the mode of ignorance.

यदा सत्त्वे प्रवृद्धे तु प्रलयं याति देहभृत् ।

तदोत्तमविदां लोकानमलान्प्रतिपद्यते

॥ १४-१४॥

रजसि प्रलयं गत्वा कर्मसङ्गिषु जायते ।

तथा प्रलीनस्तमसि मूढयोनिषु जायते

॥ १४-१५॥

Those who die with predominance of sattva reach the pure abodes (which are free from rajas and tamas) of the learned. Those who die with prevalence of the mode of passion are born among people driven by work, while those dying in the mode of ignorance take birth in the animal kingdom.

कर्मणः सुकृतस्याहुः सात्त्विकं निर्मलं फलम् ।

रजसस्तु फलं दुःखमज्ञानं तमसः फलम्

॥ १४-१६॥

It is said the fruit of actions performed in the mode of goodness bestow pure results. Actions done in the mode of passion result in pain, while those performed in the mode of ignorance result in darkness.

सत्त्वात्सञ्जायते ज्ञानं रजसो लोभ एव च ।

प्रमादमोहौ तमसो भवतोऽज्ञानमेव च

॥ १४-१७॥

From the mode of goodness arises knowledge, from the mode of passion arises greed, and from the mode of ignorance arise negligence and delusion.

ऊर्ध्वं गच्छन्ति सत्त्वस्था मध्ये तिष्ठन्ति राजसाः ।

जघन्यगुणवृत्तिस्था अधो गच्छन्ति तामसाः

॥ १४-१८॥

Those situated in the mode of goodness rise upward; those in the mode of passion stay in the middle; and those in the mode of ignorance go downward.

नान्यं गुणेभ्यः कर्तारं यदा द्रष्टानुपश्यति ।

गुणेभ्यश्च परं वेत्ति मद्भावं सोऽधिगच्छति

॥ १४-१९॥

When wise persons see that in all works there are no agents of action other than the three guṇas, and they know me to be transcendental to these guṇas, they attain my divine nature.

गुणानेतानतीत्य त्रीन्देही देहसमुद्भवान् ।

जन्ममृत्युजरादुःखैर्विमुक्तोऽमृतमश्नुते

॥ १४-२० ॥

By transcending the three modes of material nature associated with the body, one becomes free from birth, death, disease, old age, and misery, and attains immortality.

अर्जुन उवाच ।

कैर्लिङ्गैस्त्रीन्गुणानेतानतीतो भवति प्रभो ।

किमाचारः कथं चैतांस्त्रीन्गुणानतिवर्तते

॥ १४-२१ ॥

Arjun inquired: What are the characteristics of those who have gone beyond the three guṇas, O Lord? How do they act? How do they go beyond the bondage of the guṇas?

श्रीभगवानुवाच ।

प्रकाशं च प्रवृत्तिं च मोहमेव च पाण्डव ।

न द्वेष्टि सम्प्रवृत्तानि न निवृत्तानि काङ्क्षति
॥ १४-२२॥

उदासीनवदासीनो गुणैर्यो न विचाल्यते ।

गुणा वर्तन्त इत्येवं योऽवतिष्ठति नेङ्गते
॥ १४-२३॥

The Supreme Divine Personality said: O Arjun, The persons who are transcendental to the three guṇas neither hate illumination (which is born of sattva), nor activity (which is born of rajas), nor even delusion (which is born of tamas), when these are abundantly present, nor do they long for them when they are absent. They remain neutral to the modes of nature and are not disturbed by them. Knowing it is only the guṇas that act, they stay established in the self, without wavering.

समदुःखसुखः स्वस्थः समलोष्टाश्मकाञ्चनः ।

तुल्यप्रियाप्रियो धीरस्तुल्यनिन्दात्मसंस्तुतिः

॥ १४-२४॥

मानापमानयोस्तुल्यस्तुल्यो मित्रारिपक्षयोः ।

सर्वारम्भपरित्यागी गुणातीतः स उच्यते

॥ १४-२५॥

Those who are alike in happiness and distress; who are established in the self; who look upon a clod, a stone, and a piece of gold as of equal value; who remain the same amidst pleasant and unpleasant events; who are intelligent; who accept both blame and praise with equanimity; who remain the same in honor and dishonor; who treat both friend and foe alike; and who have abandoned all enterprises – they are said to have risen above the three guṇas.

मां च योऽव्यभिचारेण भक्तियोगेन सेवते ।

स गुणान्समतीत्यैतान्ब्रह्मभूयाय कल्पते

॥ १४-२६॥

Those who serve me with unalloyed devotion rise above the three modes of material nature and come to the level of Brahman.

ब्रह्मणो हि प्रतिष्ठाहममृतस्याव्ययस्य च ।

शाश्वतस्य च धर्मस्य सुखस्यैकान्तिकस्य च

॥ १४-२७॥

I am the basis of the formless Brahman, the immortal and imperishable, of eternal dharma, and of unending divine bliss.

ॐ तत्सदिति श्रीमद्भगवद्गीतासूपनिषत्सु

ब्रह्मविद्यायां योगशास्त्रे श्रीकृष्णार्जुनसंवादे

गुणत्रयविभागयोगो नाम चतुर्दशोऽध्यायः

॥ १४॥

अथ पञ्चदशोऽध्यायः । पुरुषोत्तमयोगः

HERE ENDS CHAPTER XIV OF THE BHAGAVAD-GITA.

CHAPTER XV

In this chapter, Shree Krishna explains this material world in a graphic manner, to help Arjun develop detachment from it. He compares the material world to an upside down aśhvatth tree (sacred fig). The embodied soul wanders up and down the branches of the tree, from lifetime to lifetime, without comprehending from where it originated, how long it has existed, and how it keeps growing.

The roots of the tree are above, as it has its source in God. The fruitive activities described in the Vedas are like its leaves. The tree is irrigated by the three modes of material nature. These modes create sense objects that are like the buds on the tree. The buds sprout aerial roots that engender furthe growth of the tree.
The chapter describes this symbolism in detail, to convey the idea of how the embodied soul suffering in this material world only keeps perpetuating its bondage here, in ignorance of the nature of this tree of material existence.

Finding the source, we must surrender to Him in the manner described in this chapter, and then will attain the divine Abode of God, from where we will not return to the material world again.

श्रीभगवानुवाच ।

ऊर्ध्वमूलमधःशाखमश्वत्थं प्राहुरव्ययम् ।

छन्दांसि यस्य पर्णानि यस्तं वेद स वेदवित्

॥ १५-१॥

The Supreme Divine Personality said: They speak of an eternal aśhvatth tree with its roots above and branches below. Its leaves are the Vedic hymns, and one who knows the secret of this tree is the knower of the Vedas.

अधश्चोर्ध्वं प्रसृतास्तस्य शाखा

गुणप्रवृद्धा विषयप्रवालाः ।

अधश्च मूलान्यनुसन्ततानि

कर्मानुबन्धीनि मनुष्यलोके

॥ १५-२॥

The branches of the tree extend upward and downward, nourished by the three guṇas, with the objects of the senses as tender buds. The roots of the tree hang downward, causing the flow of karma in the human form. Below, its roots branch out causing (karmic) actions in the world of humans.

न रूपमस्येह तथोपलभ्यते

नान्तो न चादिर्न च सम्प्रतिष्ठा ।

अश्वत्थमेनं सुविरूढमूलं

असङ्गशस्त्रेण दृढेन छित्त्वा

॥ १५-३ ॥

ततः पदं तत्परिमार्गितव्यं

यस्मिन्गता न निवर्तन्ति भूयः ।

तमेव चाद्यं पुरुषं प्रपद्ये ।

यतः प्रवृत्तिः प्रसृता पुराणी

॥ १५-४ ॥

The real form of this tree is not perceived in this world, neither its beginning nor end, nor its continued existence. But this deep-rooted ashvatth tree must be cut down with a strong axe of detachment. Then one must search out the base of the tree, which is the Supreme Lord, from whom streamed forth the activity of the universe a long time ago. Upon taking refuge in Him, one will not return to this world again.

निर्मानमोहा जितसङ्गदोषा

अध्यात्मनित्या विनिवृत्तकामाः ।

द्वन्द्वैर्विमुक्ताः सुखदुःखसंज्ञैर्-

गच्छन्त्यमूढाः पदमव्ययं तत्

॥ १५-५॥

Those who are free from vanity and delusion, who have overcome the evil of attachment, who dwell constantly in the self and God, who are freed from the desire to enjoy the senses, and are beyond the dualities of pleasure and pain, such liberated personalities attain My eternal Abode.

न तद्भासयते सूर्यो न शशाङ्को न पावकः ।

यद्गत्वा न निवर्तन्ते तद्धाम परमं मम

॥ १५-६॥

Neither the sun nor the moon, nor fire can illumine that Supreme Abode of Mine. Having gone There, one does not return to this material world again.

ममैवांशो जीवलोके जीवभूतः सनातनः ।

मनःषष्ठानीन्द्रियाणि प्रकृतिस्थानि कर्षति

॥ १५-७॥

The embodied souls in this material world are My eternal fragmental parts. But bound by material nature, they are struggling with the six senses including the mind.

शरीरं यदवाप्नोति यच्चाप्युत्क्रामतीश्वरः ।

गृहीत्वैतानि संयाति वायुर्गन्धानिवाशयात्

॥ १५-८॥

As the air carries fragrance from place to place, so does the embodied soul carry the mind and senses with it, when it leaves an old body and enters a new one.

श्रोत्रं चक्षुः स्पर्शनं च रसनं घ्राणमेव च ।

अधिष्ठाय मनश्चायं विषयानुपसेवते

॥ १५-९॥

Using the sense perceptions of the ears, eyes, skin, tongue, and nose, which are grouped around the mind, the embodied soul savors the objects of the senses.

उत्क्रामन्तं स्थितं वापि भुञ्जानं वा गुणान्वितम् ।
विमूढा नानुपश्यन्ति पश्यन्ति ज्ञानचक्षुषः

॥ १५-१०॥

The ignorant do not perceive the soul as it resides in the body, and as it enjoys sense objects; nor do they perceive it when it departs. But those who possess the eyes of knowledge can behold it.

यतन्तो योगिनश्चैनं पश्यन्त्यात्मन्यवस्थितम् ।
यतन्तोऽप्यकृतात्मानो नैनं पश्यन्त्यचेतसः

॥ १५-११॥

Striving yogis too are able to realize the soul enshrined in the body. However, those whose minds are not purified cannot cognize it, even though they strive to do so.

यदादित्यगतं तेजो जगद्भासयतेऽखिलम् ।
यच्चन्द्रमसि यच्चाग्नौ तत्तेजो विद्धि मामकम्

॥ १५-१२॥

Know that I am like the brilliance of the sun that illuminates the entire solar system. The radiance of the moon and the brightness of the fire also come from Me.

गामाविश्य च भूतानि धारयाम्यहमोजसा ।
पुष्णामि चौषधीः सर्वाः सोमो भूत्वा रसात्मकः

॥ १५-१३॥

Permeating the earth, I nourish all living beings with My energy. Becoming the moon, I nourish all plants with the juice of life.

अहं वैश्वानरो भूत्वा प्राणिनां देहमाश्रितः ।
प्राणापानसमायुक्तः पचाम्यन्नं चतुर्विधम्

॥ १५-१४॥

It is I who take the form of the fire of digestion in the stomachs of all living beings, and combine with the incoming and outgoing breaths, to digest and assimilate the four kinds of foods.

सर्वस्य चाहं हृदि सन्निविष्टो

मत्तः स्मृतिर्ज्ञानमपोहनञ्च ।

वेदैश्च सर्वैरहमेव वेद्य

वेदान्तकृद्वेदविदेव चाहम्

॥ १५-१५॥

I am seated in the hearts of all living beings, and from Me come memory, knowledge, as well as forgetfulness. I alone am to be known by all the Vedas, am the author of the Vedānt, and the knower of the meaning of the Vedas.

द्वाविमौ पुरुषौ लोके क्षरश्चाक्षर एव च ।

क्षरः सर्वाणि भूतानि कूटस्थोऽक्षर उच्यते

॥ १५-१६॥

There are two kinds of beings in creation, the kṣhar (perishable) and the akṣhar (imperishable). The perishable are all beings in the material realm. The imperishable are the the liberated beings.

उत्तमः पुरुषस्त्वन्यः परमात्मेत्युदाहृतः ।

यो लोकत्रयमाविश्य बिभर्त्यव्यय ईश्वरः

॥ १५-१७॥

Besides these, is the Supreme Divine Personality, who is the indestructible Supreme Soul. He enters the three worlds as the unchanging controller and supports all living beings.

यस्मात्क्षरमतीतोऽहमक्षरादपि चोत्तमः ।

अतोऽस्मि लोके वेदे च प्रथितः पुरुषोत्तमः

॥ १५-१८॥

I am transcendental to the perishable world of matter, and even to the imperishable soul; hence I am celebrated, both in the Vedas and the Smṛitis, as the Supreme Divine Personality.

यो मामेवमसम्मूढो जानाति पुरुषोत्तमम् ।

स सर्वविद्भजति मां सर्वभावेन भारत

॥ १५-१९॥

Those who know Me without doubt as the Supreme Divine Personality truly have complete knowledge. O Arjun, they worship Me with their whole being.

इति गुह्यतमं शास्त्रमिदमुक्तं मयानघ ।
एतदबुद्ध्वा बुद्धिमान्स्यात्कृतकृत्यश्च भारत
॥ १५-२०॥

I have shared this most secret principle of the Vedic scriptures with you, O sinless Arjun. By understanding this, a person becomes enlightened, and fulfills all that is to be accomplished.

ॐ तत्सदिति श्रीमद्भगवद्गीतासूपनिषत्सु
ब्रह्मविद्यायां योगशास्त्रे श्रीकृष्णार्जुन संवादे
पुरुषोत्तमयोगो नाम पञ्चदशोऽध्यायः
॥ १५॥

अथ षोडशोऽध्यायः । दैवासुरसम्पद्विभागयोगः

HERE ENDS CHAPTER XV OF THE BHAGAVAD-GITA.

CHAPTER XVI

In this chapter, Shree Krishna describes the two kinds of natures amongst human beings—the saintly and the demoniac. The saintly nature develops by following the instructions of the scriptures, cultivating the mode of goodness, and purifying the mind through spiritual practices. It leads to the enhancement of daivī sampatti (godly qualities), eventually culminating in God-realization. In contrast, there is also the demoniac nature that develops from associating with the modes of passion and ignorance, and embracing materialistic views. It breeds unwholesome traits in one's personality, and eventually throws the soul into hellish kinds of existence.

The chapter begins by describing the saintly virtues of those endowed with a divine nature. It then goes on to describe the demoniac qualities that must be scrupulously shunned because they drag the soul further into ignorance and the samsara of life and death. Shree Krishna concludes the chapter by saying that the scriptures should be our authority in determining what should be done and what should not be done. We must understand these scriptural injunctions and then perform our actions in this world accordingly.

श्रीभगवानुवाच ।

अभयं सत्त्वसंशुद्धिर्ज्ञानयोगव्यवस्थितिः ।

दानं दमश्च यज्ञश्च स्वाध्यायस्तप आर्जवम्

॥ १६-१॥

अहिंसा सत्यमक्रोधस्त्यागः शान्तिरपैशुनम् ।

दया भूतेष्वलोलुप्त्वं मार्दवं ह्रीरचापलम्

॥ १६-२॥

तेजः क्षमा धृतिः शौचमद्रोहो नातिमानिता ।

भवन्ति सम्पदं दैवीमभिजातस्य भारत

॥ १६-३॥

The Supreme Divine Personality said: O scion of Bharat, these are the saintly virtues of those endowed with a divine nature—fearlessness, purity of mind, steadfastness in spiritual knowledge, charity, control of the senses, performance of sacrifice, study of the sacred books, austerity, and straightforwardness; non-violence, truthfulness, absence of anger, renunciation, peacefulness, restraint from fault-finding, compassion toward all living beings, absence of covetousness, gentleness, modesty, and lack of fickleness; vigor, forgiveness, fortitude, cleanliness, bearing enmity toward none, and absence of vanity.

दम्भो दर्पोऽभिमानश्च क्रोधः पारुष्यमेव च ।
अज्ञानं चाभिजातस्य पार्थ सम्पदमासुरीम्

॥ १६-४॥

O Parth, the qualities of those who possess a demoniac nature are hypocrisy, arrogance, conceit, anger, harshness, and ignorance.

दैवी सम्पद्विमोक्षाय निबन्धायासुरी मता ।
मा शुचः सम्पदं दैवीमभिजातोऽसि पाण्डव

॥ १६-५॥

The divine qualities lead to liberation, while the demoniac qualities are the cause for a continuing destiny of bondage. Grieve not, O Arjun, as you were born with saintly virtues.

द्वौ भूतसर्गौ लोकेऽस्मिन्दैव आसुर एव च ।
दैवो विस्तरशः प्रोक्त आसुरं पार्थ मे शृणु

॥ १६-६॥

There are two kinds of beings in this world—those endowed with a divine nature and those possessing a demoniac nature. I have described the divine qualities in detail, O Arjun. Now hear from me about the demoniac nature.

प्रवृत्तिं च निवृत्तिं च जना न विदुरासुराः ।
न शौचं नापि चाचारो न सत्यं तेषु विद्यते

॥ १६-७॥

Those possessing a demoniac nature do not comprehend what actions are proper and what are improper. Hence, they possess neither purity, nor good conduct, nor even truthfulness.

असत्यमप्रतिष्ठं ते जगदाहुरनीश्वरम् ।
अपरस्परसम्भूतं किमन्यत्कामहैतुकम्

॥ १६-८॥

They say, "The world is without absolute truth, without any basis (for moral order), and without a God (who has created or is controlling it). It is created from the combination of the two sexes, and has no purpose other than sexual gratification."

एतां दृष्टिमवष्टभ्य नष्टात्मानोऽल्पबुद्धयः ।
प्रभवन्त्युग्रकर्माणः क्षयाय जगतोऽहिताः

॥ १६-९॥

Holding fast to such views, these misdirected souls, with small intellect and cruel actions, arise as enemies of the world threatening its destruction.

काममाश्रित्य दुष्पूरं दम्भमानमदान्विताः ।

मोहाद्गृहीत्वासद्ग्राहान्प्रवर्तन्तेऽशुचिव्रताः

॥ १६-१० ॥

Harboring insatiable lust, full of hypocrisy, pride and arrogance, the demoniac cling to their false tenets. Thus illusioned, they are attracted to the impermanent and work with impure resolve.

चिन्तामपरिमेयां च प्रलयान्तामुपाश्रिताः ।

कामोपभोगपरमा एतावदिति निश्चिताः

॥ १६-११ ॥

They are obsessed with endless anxieties that end only with death. Still, they maintain with complete assurance that gratification of desires and accumulation of wealth is the highest purpose of life.

आशापाशशतैर्बद्धाः कामक्रोधपरायणाः ।

ईहन्ते कामभोगार्थमन्यायेनार्थसञ्चयान्

॥ १६-१२॥

Held in bondage by hundreds of desires, and driven by lust and anger, they strive to accumulate wealth by unjust means, all for the gratification of their senses.

इदमद्य मया लब्धमिमं प्राप्स्ये मनोरथम् ।

इदमस्तीदमपि मे भविष्यति पुनर्धनम्

॥ १६-१३॥

असौ मया हतः शत्रुर्हनिष्ये चापरानपि ।

ईश्वरोऽहमहं भोगी सिद्धोऽहं बलवान्सुखी

॥ १६-१४॥

आढ्योऽभिजनवानस्मि कोऽन्योऽस्ति सदृशो मया ।

यक्ष्ये दास्यामि मोदिष्य इत्यज्ञानविमोहिताः

॥ १६-१५॥

The demoniac persons think, "I have gained so much wealth today, and I shall now fulfill this desire of mine. This is mine, and tomorrow I shall have even more. That enemy has been destroyed by me, and I shall destroy the others too! I am like God himself, I am the enjoyer, I am powerful, and I am happy. I am wealthy and I have highly placed relatives. Who else is equal to me? I shall perform sacrifices (to the celestial gods); I shall give alms; I shall rejoice." In this way, they are deluded by ignorance.

अनेकचित्तविभ्रान्ता मोहजालसमावृताः ।

प्रसक्ताः कामभोगेषु पतन्ति नरकेऽशुचौ

॥ १६-१६॥

Possessed and led astray by such imaginings, enveloped in a mesh of delusion, and addicted to the gratification of sensuous pleasures, they descend to the murkiest hell.

आत्मसम्भाविताः स्तब्धा धनमानमदान्विताः ।

यजन्ते नामयज्ञैस्ते दम्भेनाविधिपूर्वकम्

॥ १६-१७॥

Such self-conceited and stubborn people, full of pride and arrogant in their wealth, perform ostentatious sacrifices in name only, with no regard to the rules of the scriptures.

अहङ्कारं बलं दर्पं कामं क्रोधं च संश्रिताः ।

मामात्मपरदेहेषु प्रद्विषन्तोऽभ्यसूयकाः

॥ १६-१८॥

Blinded by egotism, strength, arrogance, desire, and anger, the demonic abuse my presence within their own body and in the bodies of others.

तानहं द्विषतः क्रूरान्संसारेषु नराधमान् ।

क्षिपाम्यजस्रमशुभानासुरीष्वेव योनिषु

॥ १६-१९॥

आसुरीं योनिमापन्ना मूढा जन्मनि जन्मनि ।

मामप्राप्यैव कौन्तेय ततो यान्त्यधमां गतिम्

॥ १६-२०॥

These cruel and hateful persons, the vile and vicious of humankind, I constantly hurl into the wombs of those with similar demoniac natures in the cycle of rebirth in the material world. These ignorant souls take birth again and again in demoniac wombs. Failing to reach me, O Arjun, they gradually sink to the most abominable type of existence.

त्रिविधं नरकस्येदं द्वारं नाशनमात्मनः ।

कामः क्रोधस्तथा लोभस्तस्मादेतत्त्रयं त्यजेत्

॥ १६-२१॥

There are three gates leading to the hell of self-destruction for the soul—lust, anger, and greed. Therefore, all should abandon these three.

एतैर्विमुक्तः कौन्तेय तमोद्वारैस्त्रिभिर्नरः ।
आचरत्यात्मनः श्रेयस्ततो याति परां गतिम्

॥ १६-२२॥

Those who are freed from the three gates to darkness endeavor for the welfare of their soul, and thereby attain the supreme goal.

यः शास्त्रविधिमुत्सृज्य वर्तते कामकारतः ।
न स सिद्धिमवाप्नोति न सुखं न परां गतिम्

॥ १६-२३॥

Those who act under the impulse of desire, discarding the injunctions of the scriptures, attain neither perfection, nor happiness, nor the supreme goal in life.

तस्माच्छास्त्रं प्रमाणं ते कार्याकार्यव्यवस्थितौ ।
ज्ञात्वा शास्त्रविधानोक्तं कर्म कर्तुमिहार्हसि

॥ १६-२४॥

Therefore, let the scriptures be your authority in determining what should be done and what should not be done. Understand the scriptural injunctions and teachings, and then perform your actions in this world accordingly.

ॐ तत्सदिति श्रीमद्भगवद्गीतासूपनिषत्सु
ब्रह्मविद्यायां योगशास्त्रे श्रीकृष्णार्जुनसंवादे
दैवासुरसम्पद्विभागयोगो नाम षोडशोऽध्यायः

॥ १६ ॥

अथ सप्तदशोऽध्यायः । श्रद्धात्रयविभागयोगः

HERE ENDETH CHAPTER XVI OF THE BHAGAVAD-GITA.

CHAPTER XVII

In this seventeenth chapter, first, he discusses the topic of faith and explains that nobody is devoid of faith, for it is an inseparable aspect of human nature. But depending upon the nature of their mind, people's faith takes on a corresponding color—sāttvic, rājasic, or tāmasic.

The nature of their faith determines the quality of their life. People also prefer food according to their dispositions. Shree Krishna classifies food into three categories and discusses the impact of each of these upon us. He then moves on to the topic of sacrifice (yajña) and how, in each of the three modes of nature, sacrifice takes on different forms. The chapter moves on to the subject of austerity, and explains austerities of the body, speech, and mind.

Each of these kinds of austerity takes on a different form as influenced by the mode of goodness, passion, or ignorance. The topic of charity (dān) is then discussed, and its three-fold divisions are described.

अर्जुन उवाच ।

ये शास्त्रविधिमुत्सृज्य यजन्ते श्रद्धयान्विताः ।

तेषां निष्ठा तु का कृष्ण सत्त्वमाहो रजस्तमः

॥ १७-१॥

Arjun said: O Krishna, where do they stand who disregard the injunctions of the scriptures, but still worship with faith? Is their faith in the mode of goodness, passion, or ignorance?

श्रीभगवानुवाच ।

त्रिविधा भवति श्रद्धा देहिनां सा स्वभावजा ।

सात्त्विकी राजसी चैव तामसी चेति तां शृणु

॥ १७-२॥

The Supreme Divine Personality said: Every human being is born with innate faith, which can be of three kinds—sāttvic, rājasic, or tāmasic. Now hear about this from me.

सत्त्वानुरूपा सर्वस्य श्रद्धा भवति भारत ।

श्रद्धामयोऽयं पुरुषो यो यच्छ्रद्धः स एव सः

॥ १७-३॥

The faith of all humans conforms to the nature of their mind. All people possess faith, and whatever the nature of their faith, that is verily what they are.

यजन्ते सात्त्विका देवान्यक्षरक्षांसि राजसाः ।

प्रेतान्भूतगणांश्चान्ये यजन्ते तामसा जनाः

॥ १७-४॥

Those in the mode of goodness worship the celestial gods; those in the mode of passion worship the yakṣhas and rākṣhasas; those in the mode of ignorance worship ghosts and spirits.

अशास्त्रविहितं घोरं तप्यन्ते ये तपो जनाः ।

दम्भाहङ्कारसंयुक्ताः कामरागबलान्विताः

॥ १७-५॥

कर्षयन्तः शरीरस्थं भूतग्राममचेतसः ।

मां चैवान्तःशरीरस्थं तान्विद्ध्यासुरनिश्चयान्

॥ १७-६॥

Some people perform stern austerities that are not enjoined by the scriptures, but rather motivated by hypocrisy and egotism. Impelled by desire and attachment, they torment not only the elements of their body, but also I who dwell within them as the Supreme Soul. Know these senseless people to be of demoniacal resolves.

आहारस्त्वपि सर्वस्य त्रिविधो भवति प्रियः ।

यज्ञस्तपस्तथा दानं तेषां भेदमिमं शृणु

॥ १७-७॥

The food persons prefer is according to their dispositions. The same is true for the sacrifice, austerity, and charity they incline toward. Now hear of the distinctions from me.

आयुःसत्त्वबलारोग्यसुखप्रीतिविवर्धनाः ।
रस्याः स्निग्धाः स्थिरा हृद्या आहाराः सात्त्विकप्रियाः

॥ १७-८॥

Persons in the mode of goodness prefer foods that promote the life span, and increase virtue, strength, health, happiness, and satisfaction. Such foods are juicy, succulent, nourishing, and naturally tasteful.

कट्वम्ललवणात्युष्णतीक्ष्णरूक्षविदाहिनः ।
आहारा राजसस्येष्टा दुःखशोकामयप्रदाः

॥ १७-९॥

Foods that are too bitter, too sour, salty, very hot, pungent, dry, and chiliful, are dear to persons in the mode of passion. Such foods produce pain, grief, and disease.

यातयामं गतरसं पूति पर्युषितं च यत् ।
उच्छिष्टमपि चामेध्यं भोजनं तामसप्रियम्

॥ १७-१०॥

Foods that are overcooked, stale, putrid, polluted, and impure are dear to persons in the mode of ignorance.

अफलाकाङ्क्षिभिर्यज्ञो विधिदृष्टो य इज्यते ।

यष्टव्यमेवेति मनः समाधाय स सात्त्विकः

॥ १७-११॥

Sacrifice that is performed according to the scriptural injunctions without expectation of rewards, with the firm conviction of the mind that it is a matter of duty is of the nature of goodness.

अभिसन्धाय तु फलं दम्भार्थमपि चैव यत् ।

इज्यते भरतश्रेष्ठ तं यज्ञं विद्धि राजसम्

॥ १७-१२॥

O best of the Bharatas, know that sacrifice, which is performed for material benefit, or with hypocritical aim, to be in the mode of passion.

विधिहीनमसृष्टान्नं मन्त्रहीनमदक्षिणम् ।

श्रद्धाविरहितं यज्ञं तामसं परिचक्षते

॥ १७-१३॥

Sacrifice devoid of faith and contrary to the injunctions of the scriptures, in which no food is offered, no mantras chanted, and no donation made, is to be considered in the mode of ignorance.

देवद्विजगुरुप्राज्ञपूजनं शौचमार्जवम् ।
ब्रह्मचर्यमहिंसा च शारीरं तप उच्यते

॥ १७-१४॥

Worship of the Supreme Lord, the Brahmins, the spiritual master, the wise, and the elders—when this is done with the observance of cleanliness, simplicity, celibacy, and non-violence—is declared as the austerity of the body.

अनुद्वेगकरं वाक्यं सत्यं प्रियहितं च यत् ।
स्वाध्यायाभ्यसनं चैव वाङ्मयं तप उच्यते

॥ १७-१५॥

Words that do not cause distress, are truthful, inoffensive, and beneficial, as well as the regular recitation of the Vedic scriptures—these are declared as the austerity of speech.

मनः प्रसादः सौम्यत्वं मौनमात्मविनिग्रहः ।
भावसंशुद्धिरित्येतत्तपो मानसमुच्यते

॥ १७-१६॥

Serenity of thought, gentleness, silence, self-control, and purity of purpose—all these are declared as the austerity of the mind.

श्रद्धया परया तप्तं तपस्तत्त्रिविधं नरैः ।
अफलाकाङ्क्षिभिर्युक्तैः सात्त्विकं परिचक्षते

॥ १७-१७॥

When devout persons with ardent faith practice these three-fold austerities without yearning for material rewards, they are designated as austerities in the mode of goodness.

सत्कारमानपूजार्थं तपो दम्भेन चैव यत् ।
क्रियते तदिह प्रोक्तं राजसं चलमध्रुवम्

॥ १७-१८॥

Austerity that is performed with ostentation for the sake of gaining honor, respect, and adoration is in the mode of passion. Its benefits are unstable and transitory.

मूढग्राहेणात्मनो यत्पीडया क्रियते तपः ।
परस्योत्सादनार्थं वा तत्तामसमुदाहृतम्

॥ १७-१९॥

Austerity that is performed by those with confused notions, and which involves torturing the self or harming others, is described to be in the mode of ignorance.

दातव्यमिति यद्दानं दीयतेऽनुपकारिणे ।
देशे काले च पात्रे च तद्दानं सात्त्विकं स्मृतम्

॥ १७-२०॥

Charity given to a worthy person simply because it is right to give, without consideration of anything in return, at the proper time and in the proper place, is stated to be in the mode of goodness.

यत्तु प्रत्युपकारार्थं फलमुद्दिश्य वा पुनः ।
दीयते च परिक्लिष्टं तद्दानं राजसं स्मृतम्

॥ १७-२१॥

But charity given with reluctance, with the hope of a return or in expectation of a reward, is said to be in the mode of passion.

अदेशकाले यद्दानमपात्रेभ्यश्च दीयते ।
असत्कृतमवज्ञातं तत्तामसमुदाहृतम्

॥ १७-२२॥

And that charity, which is given at the wrong place and wrong time to unworthy persons, without showing respect, or with contempt, is held to be of the nature of nescience.

ॐतत्सदिति निर्देशो ब्रह्मणस्त्रिविधः स्मृतः ।

ब्राह्मणास्तेन वेदाश्च यज्ञाश्च विहिताः पुरा

॥ १७-२३॥

The words "Om Tat Sat" have been declared as symbolic representations of the Supreme Absolute Truth, from the beginning of creation. From them came the priests, scriptures, and sacrifice.

तस्मादोमित्युदाहृत्य यज्ञदानतपःक्रियाः ।

प्रवर्तन्ते विधानोक्ताः सततं ब्रह्मवादिनाम्

॥ १७-२४॥

Therefore, when performing acts of sacrifice, offering charity, or undertaking penance, expounders of the Vedas always begin by uttering "Om" according to the prescriptions of Vedic injunctions.

तदित्यनभिसन्धाय फलं यज्ञतपःक्रियाः ।
दानक्रियाश्च विविधाः क्रियन्ते मोक्षकाङ्क्षिभिः

॥ १७-२५॥

Persons who do not desire fruitive rewards, but seek to be free from material entanglements, utter the word "Tat" along with acts of austerity, sacrifice, and charity.

सद्भावे साधुभावे च सदित्येतत्प्रयुज्यते ।
प्रशस्ते कर्मणि तथा सच्छब्दः पार्थ युज्यते

॥ १७-२६॥

यज्ञे तपसि दाने च स्थितिः सदिति चोच्यते ।
कर्म चैव तदर्थीयं सदित्येवाभिधीयते

॥ १७-२७॥

The word "Sat" means eternal existence and goodness. O Arjun, it is also used to describe an auspicious action. Being established in the performance of sacrifice, penance, and charity, is also described by the word "Sat." And so any act for such purposes is named "Sat."

अश्रद्धया हुतं दत्तं तपस्तप्तं कृतं च यत् ।

असदित्युच्यते पार्थ न च तत्प्रेत्य नो इह

॥ १७-२८॥

O son of Pritha, whatever acts of sacrifice or penance are done without faith, are termed as "Asat." They are useless both in this world and the next.

ॐ तत्सदिति श्रीमद्भगवद्गीतासूपनिषत्सु

ब्रह्मविद्यायां योगशास्त्रे श्रीकृष्णार्जुनसंवादे

श्रद्धात्रयविभागयोगो नाम सप्तदशोऽध्यायः

॥ १७॥

अथाष्टादशोऽध्यायः । मोक्षसंन्यासयोगः

HERE ENDETH CHAPTER XVII OF THE BHAGAVAD-GITA.

CHAPTER XVIII

The final chapter of the Bhagavad Gita is the longest and covers many subjects. Arjun initiates the topic of renunciation with a question about two commonly used Sanskrit words, sanyās (renunciation of actions) and tyāg (renunciation of desires). Both words come from roots words meaning "to abandon."

He establishes that those with deficient understanding see themselves as the only cause of their works. But the enlightened souls, with purified intellect, neither consider themselves as the doer nor the enjoyer of their actions.

The chapter then goes on to paint a picture of those who have attained perfection in spiritual life and are situated in Brahman-realization. It adds that even such perfect yogis find completion in their realization by engaging in bhakti. Thus, the secret of the Supreme Divine Personality can only be known through loving devotion.

अर्जुन उवाच ।

संन्यासस्य महाबाहो तत्त्वमिच्छामि वेदितुम् ।

त्यागस्य च हृषीकेश पृथक्केशिनिषूदन

॥ १८-१॥

Arjun said: O mighty-armed Krishna, I wish to understand the nature of sanyās (renunciation of actions) and tyāg (renunciation of the desire for the fruits of actions). O Hrishikesh, I also wish to know the distinction between the two, O Keshinisudan.

श्रीभगवानुवाच ।

काम्यानां कर्मणां न्यासं संन्यासं कवयो विदुः ।

सर्वकर्मफलत्यागं प्राहुस्त्यागं विचक्षणाः

॥ १८-२॥

The Supreme Divine Personality said: Giving up of actions motivated by desire is what the wise understand as sanyās. Relinquishing the fruits of all actions is what the learned declare to be tyāg.

त्याज्यं दोषवदित्येके कर्म प्राहुर्मनीषिणः ।

यज्ञदानतपःकर्म न त्याज्यमिति चापरे

॥ १८-३॥

Some learned people declare that all kinds of actions should be given up as evil, while others maintain that acts of sacrifice, charity, and penance should never be abandoned.

निश्चयं शृणु मे तत्र त्यागे भरतसत्तम ।

त्यागो हि पुरुषव्याघ्र त्रिविधः सम्प्रकीर्तितः

॥ १८-४॥

Now hear my conclusion on the subject of renunciation, O tiger amongst men, for renunciation has been declared to be of three kinds.

यज्ञदानतपःकर्म न त्याज्यं कार्यमेव तत् ।

यज्ञो दानं तपश्चैव पावनानि मनीषिणाम्

॥ १८-५॥

Actions based upon sacrifice, charity, and penance should never be abandoned; they must certainly be performed. Indeed, acts of sacrifice, charity, and penance are purifying even for those who are wise.

एतान्यपि तु कर्माणि सङ्गं त्यक्त्वा फलानि च ।
कर्तव्यानीति मे पार्थ निश्चितं मतमुत्तमम्

॥ १८-६॥

These activities must be performed without attachment and expectation for rewards. This is my definite and supreme verdict, O Arjun.

नियतस्य तु संन्यासः कर्मणो नोपपद्यते ।
मोहात्तस्य परित्यागस्तामसः परिकीर्तितः

॥ १८-७॥

Prescribed duties should never be renounced. Such deluded renunciation is said to be in the mode of ignorance.

दुःखमित्येव यत्कर्म कायक्लेशभयात्त्यजेत् ।
स कृत्वा राजसं त्यागं नैव त्यागफलं लभेत्

॥ १८-८॥

To give up prescribed duties because they are troublesome or cause bodily discomfort is renunciation in the mode of passion. Such renunciation is never beneficial or elevating.

कार्यमित्येव यत्कर्म नियतं क्रियतेऽर्जुन ।
सङ्गं त्यक्त्वा फलं चैव स त्यागः सात्त्विको मतः

॥ १८-९॥

When actions are taken in response to duty, Arjun, and one relinquishes attachment to any reward, it is considered renunciation in the nature of goodness.

न द्वेष्ट्यकुशलं कर्म कुशले नानुषज्जते ।
त्यागी सत्त्वसमाविष्टो मेधावी छिन्नसंशयः

॥ १८-१०॥

Those who neither avoid disagreeable work nor seek work because it is agreeable are persons of true renunciation. They are endowed with the quality of the mode of goodness and have no doubts (about the nature of work).

न हि देहभृता शक्यं त्यक्तुं कर्माण्यशेषतः ।
यस्तु कर्मफलत्यागी स त्यागीत्यभिधीयते

॥ १८-११॥

For the embodied being, it is impossible to give up activities entirely. But those who relinquish the fruits of their actions are said to be truly renounced.

अनिष्टमिष्टं मिश्रं च त्रिविधं कर्मणः फलम् ।
भवत्यत्यागिनां प्रेत्य न तु संन्यासिनां क्वचित्
॥ १८-१२॥

The three-fold fruits of actions—pleasant, unpleasant, and mixed—accrue even after death to those who are attached to personal reward. But, for those who renounce the fruits of their actions, there are no such results in the here or hereafter.

पञ्चैतानि महाबाहो कारणानि निबोध मे ।
साङ्ख्ये कृतान्ते प्रोक्तानि सिद्धये सर्वकर्मणाम्
॥ १८-१३॥

O Arjun, now learn from me about the five factors that have been mentioned for the accomplishment of all actions in the doctrine of Sānkhya, which explains how to stop the reactions of karmas.

अधिष्ठानं तथा कर्ता करणं च पृथग्विधम् ।
विविधाश्च पृथक्चेष्टा दैवं चैवात्र पञ्चमम्
॥ १८-१४॥

The body, the doer, the various senses, the many kinds of efforts, and Divine Providence—these are the five factors of action.

शरीरवाङ्मनोभिर्यत्कर्म प्रारभते नरः ।
न्याय्यं वा विपरीतं वा पञ्चैते तस्य हेतवः
॥ १८-१५॥

तत्रैवं सति कर्तारमात्मानं केवलं तु यः ।
पश्यत्यकृतबुद्धित्वान्न स पश्यति दुर्मतिः
॥ १८-१६॥

These five are the contributory factors for whatever action is performed, whether proper or improper, with body, speech, or mind. Those who do not understand this regard the soul as the only doer. With their impure intellects they cannot see things as they are.

यस्य नाहङ्कृतो भावो बुद्धिर्यस्य न लिप्यते ।
हत्वाऽपि स इमाँल्लोकान्न हन्ति न निबध्यते
॥ १८-१७॥

Those who are free from the ego of being the doer, and whose intellect is unattached, though they may slay living beings, they neither kill nor are they bound by actions.

ज्ञानं ज्ञेयं परिज्ञाता त्रिविधा कर्मचोदना ।

करणं कर्म कर्तेति त्रिविधः कर्मसङ्ग्रहः

॥ १८-१८॥

Knowledge, the object of knowledge, and the knower—these are the three factors that induce action. The instrument of action, the act itself, and the doer—these are the three constituents of action.

ज्ञानं कर्म च कर्ता च त्रिधैव गुणभेदतः ।

प्रोच्यते गुणसङ्ख्याने यथावच्छृणु तान्यपि

॥ १८-१९॥

Knowledge, action, and the doer are declared to be of three kinds in the Sānkhya philosophy, distinguished according to the three modes of material nature. Listen, and I will explain their distinctions to you.

सर्वभूतेषु येनैकं भावमव्ययमीक्षते ।

अविभक्तं विभक्तेषु तज्ज्ञानं विद्धि सात्त्विकम्

॥ १८-२०॥

Understand that knowledge to be in the mode of goodness by which a person sees one undivided imperishable reality within all diverse living beings.

पृथक्त्वेन तु यज्ज्ञानं नानाभावान्पृथग्विधान् ।

वेत्ति सर्वेषु भूतेषु तज्ज्ञानं विद्धि राजसम्

॥ १८-२१॥

That knowledge is to be considered in the mode of passion by which one sees the manifold living entities in diverse bodies as individual and unconnected.

यत्तु कृत्स्नवदेकस्मिन्कार्ये सक्तमहैतुकम् ।

अतत्त्वार्थवदल्पं च तत्तामसमुदाहृतम्

॥ १८-२२॥

That knowledge is said to be in the mode of ignorance where one is engrossed in a fragmental concept as if it encompasses the whole, and which is neither grounded in reason nor based on the truth.

नियतं सङ्गरहितमरागद्वेषतः कृतम् ।

अफलप्रेप्सुना कर्म यत्तत्सात्त्विकमुच्यते

॥ १८-२३॥

Action that is in accordance with the scriptures, which is free from attachment and aversion, and which is done without desire for rewards, is in the mode of goodness.

यत्तु कामेप्सुना कर्म साहङ्कारेण वा पुनः ।
क्रियते बहुलायासं तद्राजसमुदाहृतम्

॥ १८-२४॥

Action that is prompted by selfish desire, enacted with pride, and full of stress, is in the nature of passion.

अनुबन्धं क्षयं हिंसामनपेक्ष्य च पौरुषम् ।
मोहादारभ्यते कर्म यत्तत्तामसमुच्यते

॥ १८-२५॥

That action is declared to be in the mode of ignorance, which is begun out of delusion, without thought to one's own ability, and disregarding consequences, loss, and injury to others.

मुक्तसङ्गोऽनहंवादी धृत्युत्साहसमन्वितः ।
सिद्ध्यसिद्ध्योर्निर्विकारः कर्ता सात्त्विक उच्यते

॥ १८-२६॥

The performer is said to be in the mode of goodness, when he or she is free from egotism and attachment, endowed with enthusiasm and determination, and equipoised in success and failure.

रागी कर्मफलप्रेप्सुर्लुब्धो हिंसात्मकोऽशुचिः ।
हर्षशोकान्वितः कर्ता राजसः परिकीर्तितः

॥ १८-२७॥

The performer is considered in the mode of passion when he or she craves the fruits of the work, is covetous, violent-natured, impure, and moved by joy and sorrow.

अयुक्तः प्राकृतः स्तब्धः शठो नैष्कृतिकोऽलसः ।
विषादी दीर्घसूत्री च कर्ता तामस उच्यते

॥ १८-२८॥

A performer in the mode of ignorance is one who is undisciplined, vulgar, stubborn, deceitful, slothful, despondent, and procrastinating.

बुद्धेर्भेदं धृतेश्चैव गुणतस्त्रिविधं शृणु ।
प्रोच्यमानमशेषेण पृथक्त्वेन धनञ्जय

॥ १८-२९॥

Hear now, O Arjun, of the distinctions of intellect and determination, according to the three modes of material nature, as I describe them in detail.

प्रवृत्तिं च निवृत्तिं च कार्याकार्ये भयाभये ।

बन्धं मोक्षं च या वेत्ति बुद्धिः सा पार्थ सात्त्विकी

॥ १८-३०॥

The intellect is said to be in the nature of goodness, O Parth, when it understands what is proper action and what is improper action, what is duty and what is non-duty, what is to be feared and what is not to be feared, what is binding and what is liberating.

यया धर्ममधर्मं च कार्यं चाकार्यमेव च ।

अयथावत्प्रजानाति बुद्धिः सा पार्थ राजसी

॥ १८-३१॥

The intellect is considered in the mode of passion when it is confused between righteousness and unrighteousness, and cannot distinguish between right and wrong conduct.

अधर्मं धर्ममिति या मन्यते तमसावृता ।

सर्वार्थान्विपरीतांश्च बुद्धिः सा पार्थ तामसी

॥ १८-३२॥

That intellect which is shrouded in darkness, imagining irreligion to be religion, and perceiving untruth to be the truth, is of the nature of ignorance.

धृत्या यया धारयते मनःप्राणेन्द्रियक्रियाः ।
योगेनाव्यभिचारिण्या धृतिः सा पार्थ सात्त्विकी

॥ १८-३३॥

The steadfast will that is developed through Yog, and which sustains the activities of the mind, the life-airs, and the senses, is said to be determination in the mode of goodness.

यया तु धर्मकामार्थान्धृत्या धारयतेऽर्जुन ।
प्रसङ्गेन फलाकाङ्क्षी धृतिः सा पार्थ राजसी

॥ १८-३४॥

The steadfast will by which one holds to duty, pleasures, and wealth, out of attachment and desire for rewards, is determination in the mode of passion.

यया स्वप्नं भयं शोकं विषादं मदमेव च ।
न विमुञ्चति दुर्मेधा धृतिः सा पार्थ तामसी

॥ १८-३५॥

That unintelligent resolve is said to be determination in the mode of ignorance, in which one does not give up dreaming, fearing, grieving, despair, and conceit.

सुखं त्विदानीं त्रिविधं शृणु मे भरतर्षभ ।
अभ्यासाद्रमते यत्र दुःखान्तं च निगच्छति

॥ १८-३६॥

And now hear from me, O Arjun, of the three kinds of happiness in which the embodied soul rejoices, and can even reach the end of all suffering.

यत्तदग्रे विषमिव परिणामेऽमृतोपमम् ।
तत्सुखं सात्त्विकं प्रोक्तमात्मबुद्धिप्रसादजम्

॥ १८-३७॥

That which seems like poison at first, but tastes like nectar in the end, is said to be happiness in the mode of goodness. It is generated by the pure intellect that is situated in self-knowledge.

विषयेन्द्रियसंयोगाद्यत्तदग्रेऽमृतोपमम् ।
परिणामे विषमिव तत्सुखं राजसं स्मृतम्

॥ १८-३८॥

Happiness is said to be in the mode of passion when it is derived from the contact of the senses with their objects. Such happiness is like nectar at first but poison at the end.

यदग्रे चानुबन्धे च सुखं मोहनमात्मनः ।

निद्रालस्यप्रमादोत्थं तत्तामसमुदाहृतम्

॥ १८-३९॥

That happiness which covers the nature of the self from beginning to end, and which is derived from sleep, indolence, and negligence, is said to be in the mode of ignorance.

न तदस्ति पृथिव्यां वा दिवि देवेषु वा पुनः ।

सत्त्वं प्रकृतिजैर्मुक्तं यदेभिः स्यात्त्रिभिर्गुणैः

॥ १८-४०॥

No living being on earth or the higher celestial abodes in this material realm is free from the influence of these three modes of nature.

ब्राह्मणक्षत्रियविशां शूद्राणां च परन्तप ।

कर्माणि प्रविभक्तानि स्वभावप्रभवैर्गुणैः

॥ १८-४१॥

The duties of the Brahmins, Kshatriyas, Vaishyas, and Shudras—are distributed according to their qualities, in accordance with their guṇas (and not by birth).

शमो दमस्तपः शौचं क्षान्तिरार्जवमेव च ।

ज्ञानं विज्ञानमास्तिक्यं ब्रह्मकर्म स्वभावजम्

॥ १८-४२॥

Tranquility, restraint, austerity, purity, patience, integrity, knowledge, wisdom, and belief in a hereafter—these are the intrinsic qualities of work for Brahmins.

शौर्यं तेजो धृतिर्दाक्ष्यं युद्धे चाप्यपलायनम् ।

दानमीश्वरभावश्च क्षात्रं कर्म स्वभावजम्

॥ १८-४३॥

Valor, strength, fortitude, skill in weaponry, resolve never to retreat from battle, large-heartedness in charity, and leadership abilities, these are the natural qualities of work for Kshatriyas.

कृषिगौरक्ष्यवाणिज्यं वैश्यकर्म स्वभावजम् ।

परिचर्यात्मकं कर्म शूद्रस्यापि स्वभावजम्

॥ १८-४४॥

Agriculture, dairy farming, and commerce are the natural works for those with the qualities of Vaishyas. Serving through work is the natural duty for those with the qualities of Shudras.

स्वे स्वे कर्मण्यभिरतः संसिद्धिं लभते नरः ।

स्वकर्मनिरतः सिद्धिं यथा विन्दति तच्छृणु

॥ १८-४५॥

By fulfilling their duties, born of their innate qualities, human beings can attain perfection. Now hear from me how one can become perfect by discharging one's prescribed duties.

यतः प्रवृत्तिर्भूतानां येन सर्वमिदं ततम् ।

स्वकर्मणा तमभ्यर्च्य सिद्धिं विन्दति मानवः

॥ १८-४६॥

By performing one's natural occupation, one worships the Creator from whom all living entities have come into being, and by whom the whole universe is pervaded. By such performance of work, a person easily attains perfection.

श्रेयान्स्वधर्मो विगुणः परधर्मात्स्वनुष्ठितात् ।
स्वभावनियतं कर्म कुर्वन्नाप्नोति किल्बिषम्

॥ १८-४७॥

It is better to do one's own dharma, even though imperfectly, than to do another's dharma, even though perfectly. By doing one's innate duties, a person does not incur sin.

सहजं कर्म कौन्तेय सदोषमपि न त्यजेत् ।
सर्वारम्भा हि दोषेण धूमेनाग्निरिवावृताः

॥ १८-४८॥

One should not abandon duties born of one's nature, even if one sees defects in them, O son of Kunti. Indeed, all endeavors are veiled by some evil, as fire is by smoke.

असक्तबुद्धिः सर्वत्र जितात्मा विगतस्पृहः ।
नैष्कर्म्यसिद्धिं परमां संन्यासेनाधिगच्छति

॥ १८-४९॥

Those whose intellect is unattached everywhere, who have mastered the mind, and are free from desires by the practice of renunciation, attain the highest perfection of freedom from action.

सिद्धिं प्राप्तो यथा ब्रह्म तथाप्नोति निबोध मे ।

समासेनैव कौन्तेय निष्ठा ज्ञानस्य या परा

॥ १८-५०॥

Hear from me briefly, O Arjun, and I shall explain how one, who has attained perfection (of cessation of actions), can also attain Brahman by being firmly fixed in transcendental knowledge.

बुद्ध्या विशुद्धया युक्तो धृत्यात्मानं नियम्य च ।
शब्दादीन्विषयांस्त्यक्त्वा रागद्वेषौ व्युदस्य च

॥ १८-५१॥

विविक्तसेवी लघ्वाशी यतवाक्कायमानसः ।
ध्यानयोगपरो नित्यं वैराग्यं समुपाश्रितः

॥ १८-५२॥

अहङ्कारं बलं दर्पं कामं क्रोधं परिग्रहम् ।
विमुच्य निर्ममः शान्तो ब्रह्मभूयाय कल्पते

॥ १८-५३॥

One becomes fit to attain Brahman when he or she possesses a purified intellect and firmly restrains the senses, abandoning sound and other objects of the senses, casting aside attraction and aversion. Such a person relishes solitude, eats lightly, controls body, mind, and speech, is ever engaged in meditation, and practices dispassion. Free from egotism, violence, arrogance, desire, possessiveness of property, and selfishness, such a person, situated in tranquility, is fit for union with Brahman (i.e., realization of the Absolute Truth as Brahman).

ब्रह्मभूतः प्रसन्नात्मा न शोचति न काङ्क्षति ।
समः सर्वेषु भूतेषु मद्भक्तिं लभते पराम्

॥ १८-५४॥

One situated in the transcendental Brahman realization becomes mentally serene, neither grieving nor desiring. Being equitably disposed toward all living beings, such a yogi attains supreme devotion unto me.

भक्त्या मामभिजानाति यावान्यश्चास्मि तत्त्वतः ।
ततो मां तत्त्वतो ज्ञात्वा विशते तदनन्तरम्

॥ १८-५५॥

Only by loving devotion to me does one come to know who I am in truth. Then, having come to know me, my devotee enters into full consciousness of me.

सर्वकर्माण्यपि सदा कुर्वाणो मद्व्यपाश्रयः ।
मत्प्रसादादवाप्नोति शाश्वतं पदमव्ययम्

॥ १८-५६॥

My devotees, though performing all kinds of actions, take full refuge in me. By my grace, they attain the eternal and imperishable abode.

चेतसा सर्वकर्माणि मयि संन्यस्य मत्परः ।

बुद्धियोगमुपाश्रित्य मच्चित्तः सततं भव

॥ १८-५७॥

Dedicate your every activity to me, making me your supreme goal. Taking shelter of the Yog of the intellect, keep your consciousness absorbed in me always.

मच्चित्तः सर्वदुर्गाणि मत्प्रसादात्तरिष्यसि ।

अथ चेत्त्वमहङ्कारान्न श्रोष्यसि विनङ्क्ष्यसि

॥ १८-५८॥

If you remember me always, by my grace you will overcome all obstacles and difficulties. But if, due to pride, you do not listen to my advice, you will perish.

यदहङ्कारमाश्रित्य न योत्स्य इति मन्यसे ।

मिथ्यैष व्यवसायस्ते प्रकृतिस्त्वां नियोक्ष्यति

॥ १८-५९॥

If, motivated by pride, you think, “I shall not fight,” your decision will be in vain. Your own material (Kshatriya) nature will compel you to fight.

स्वभावजेन कौन्तेय निबद्धः स्वेन कर्मणा ।

कर्तुं नेच्छसि यन्मोहात्करिष्यस्यवशोऽपि तत्

॥ १८-६० ॥

O Arjun, that action which out of delusion you do not wish to do, you will be driven to do it by your own inclination, born of your own material nature.

ईश्वरः सर्वभूतानां हृद्देशेऽर्जुन तिष्ठति ।

भ्रामयन्सर्वभूतानि यन्त्रारूढानि मायया

॥ १८-६१ ॥

O Arjun, that action which out of delusion you do not wish to do, you will be driven to do it by your own inclination, born of your own material nature.

तमेव शरणं गच्छ सर्वभावेन भारत ।

तत्प्रसादात्परां शान्तिं स्थानं प्राप्स्यसि शाश्वतम्

॥ १८-६२ ॥

Surrender exclusively unto him with your whole being, O Bharat. By his grace, you will attain perfect peace and the eternal abode.

इति ते ज्ञानमाख्यातं गुह्याद्गुह्यतरं मया ।

विमृश्यैतदशेषेण यथेच्छसि तथा कुरु

॥ १८-६३॥

Thus, I have explained to you this knowledge that is more secret than all secrets. Ponder over it deeply, and then do as you wish.

सर्वगुह्यतमं भूयः शृणु मे परमं वचः ।

इष्टोऽसि मे दृढमिति ततो वक्ष्यामि ते हितम्

॥ १८-६४॥

Hear again my supreme instruction, the most confidential of all knowledge. I am revealing this for your benefit because you are very dear to me.

मन्मना भव मद्भक्तो मद्याजी मां नमस्कुरु ।

मामेवैष्यसि सत्यं ते प्रतिजाने प्रियोऽसि मे

॥ १८-६५॥

Always think of me, be devoted to me, worship me, and offer obeisance to me. Doing so, you will certainly come to me. This is my pledge to you, for you are very dear to me.

सर्वधर्मान्परित्यज्य मामेकं शरणं व्रज ।
अहं त्वा सर्वपापेभ्यो मोक्षयिष्यामि मा शुचः
॥ १८-६६॥

Abandon all varieties of dharmas and simply surrender unto me alone. I shall liberate you from all sinful reactions; do not fear.

इदं ते नातपस्काय नाभक्ताय कदाचन ।
न चाशुश्रूषवे वाच्यं न च मां योऽभ्यसूयति
॥ १८-६७॥

This instruction should never be explained to those who are not austere or to those who are not devoted. It should also not be spoken to those who are averse to listening (to spiritual topics), and especially not to those who are envious of me.

य इदं परमं गुह्यं मद्भक्तेष्वभिधास्यति ।
भक्तिं मयि परां कृत्वा मामेवैष्यत्यसंशयः
॥ १८-६८॥

Those, who teach this most confidential knowledge amongst my devotees, perform the greatest act of love. They will come to me without doubt.

न च तस्मान्मनुष्येषु कश्चिन्मे प्रियकृत्तमः ।
भविता न च मे तस्मादन्यः प्रियतरो भुवि

॥ १८-६९॥

No human being does more loving service to me than they; nor shall there ever be anyone on this earth more dear to me.

अध्येष्यते च य इमं धर्म्यं संवादमावयोः ।
ज्ञानयज्ञेन तेनाहमिष्टः स्यामिति मे मतिः

॥ १८-७०॥

And I proclaim that those who study this sacred dialogue of ours will worship me (with their intellect) through the sacrifice of knowledge; such is my view.

श्रद्धावाननसूयश्च शृणुयादपि यो नरः ।
सोऽपि मुक्तः शुभाँल्लोकान्प्राप्नुयात्पुण्यकर्मणाम्

॥ १८-७१॥

Even those who only listen to this knowledge with faith and without envy will be liberated from sins and attain the auspicious abodes where the pious dwell.

कच्चिदेतच्छ्रुतं पार्थ त्वयैकाग्रेण चेतसा ।

कच्चिदज्ञानसम्मोहः प्रनष्टस्ते धनञ्जय

॥ १८-७२॥

O Arjun, have you heard me with a concentrated mind? Have your ignorance and delusion been destroyed?

अर्जुन उवाच ।

नष्टो मोहः स्मृतिर्लब्धा त्वत्प्रसादान्मयाच्युत ।

स्थितोऽस्मि गतसन्देहः करिष्ये वचनं तव ॥ १८-७३॥

Arjun Said: O infallible one, by your grace my illusion has been dispelled, and I am situated in knowledge. I am now free from doubts, and I shall act according to your instructions.

सञ्जय उवाच ।

इत्यहं वासुदेवस्य पार्थस्य च महात्मनः ।

संवादमिममश्रौषमद्भुतं रोमहर्षणम्

॥ १८-७४॥

Sanjay said: Thus, have I heard this wonderful conversation between Shree Krishna, the son of Vasudev, and Arjun, the noble-hearted son of Pritha. So thrilling is the message that my hair is standing on end.

व्यासप्रसादाच्छ्रुतवानेतद्गुह्यमहं परम् ।

योगं योगेश्वरात्कृष्णात्साक्षात्कथयतः स्वयम्

॥ १८-७५॥

By the grace of Veda Vyas, I have heard this supreme and most secret Yog from the Lord of Yog, Shree Krishna himself.

राजन्संस्मृत्य संस्मृत्य संवादमिममद्भुतम् ।
केशवार्जुनयोः पुण्यं हृष्यामि च मुहुर्मुहुः

॥ १८-७६॥

As I repeatedly recall this astonishing and wonderful dialogue between the Supreme Lord Shree Krishna and Arjun, O King, I rejoice again and again.

तच्च संस्मृत्य संस्मृत्य रूपमत्यद्भुतं हरेः ।
विस्मयो मे महान् राजन्हृष्यामि च पुनः पुनः

॥ १८-७७॥

And remembering that most astonishing and wonderful cosmic form of Lord Krishna, great is my astonishment, and I am thrilled with joy over and over again.

यत्र योगेश्वरः कृष्णो यत्र पार्थो धनुर्धरः ।
तत्र श्रीर्विजयो भूतिर्ध्रुवा नीतिर्मतिर्मम

॥ १८-७८॥

Wherever there is Shree Krishna, the Lord of all Yog, and wherever there is Arjun, the supreme archer, there will also certainly be unending opulence, victory, prosperity, and righteousness. Of this, I am certain.

ॐ तत्सदिति श्रीमद्भगवद्गीतासूपनिषत्सु

ब्रह्मविद्यायां योगशास्त्रे श्रीकृष्णार्जुनसंवादे

मोक्षसंन्यासयोगो नाम अष्टादशोऽध्यायः

॥ १८॥

My marvel and my love and bliss. O Archer-Prince! All hail!

O Krishna, Lord of Yoga! surely there shall not fail

Blessing, and victory, and power, for Thy most mighty sake,

Where this song comes of Arjun, and how with God he spake.

HERE ENDETH CHAPTER XVIII OF THE BHAGAVAD-GITA.